13/6

D0236364

KAFKA'S CASTLE

KAFKA'S CASTLE

BY

RONALD GRAY

CAMBRIDGE
AT THE UNIVERSITY PRESS
1956

PUBLISHED BY
THE SYNDICS OF THE CAMBRIDGE UNIVERSITY PRESS

London Office: Bentley House, N.W. 1
American Branch: New York

Agents for Canada, India and Pakistan: Macmillan

Printed in the Netherlands
by Joh. Enschedé en Zonen , Haarlem

FOR PAT

ACKNOWLEDGEMENTS

I am very grateful indeed to Humphry and Molly Trevelyan for their great encouragement when I first began writing this book. I also wish to thank Harold Mason for his careful scrutiny of the manuscript. The Colloquium of the German Department in the University of Cambridge supplied valued comment.

Grateful acknowledgements are due to Messrs Schocken Books for permission to translate from Kafka's work. All quotations have been translated by me; those from *Das Schloss* are based on the third edition, published by Messrs. Schocken in New York in 1946.

CAMBRIDGE   R. D. G.
October 1955

A NOTE ON THE GERMAN AND ENGLISH EDITIONS OF 'THE CASTLE'

Readers who were first introduced to *The Castle* by Mr Edwin Muir's translation of 1930, or by any of the three later editions of it up to 1947, may be surprised to find that a great deal of the present commentary deals with passages not contained in that translation. To them some explanation is due. The first German edition, published in 1926, was fully translated by Mr Muir. The second German edition, however, apart from adding some variant readings, fragments, and deleted passages, revealed that the original manuscript did not end in the middle of chapter eighteen, but added a nineteenth and an uncompleted twentieth chapter. (Fuller details are given in chapter IX below.) The third German edition gives a further continuation of the twentieth chapter, which, however, was apparently never actually completed by the author. In the translation in the definitive edition, published in 1953 by Messrs Secker and Warburg, a slightly amended text of Mr Muir's translation is given, and the additional material has been fully translated by Eithne Wilkins and Ernst Kaiser.

English and American readers must be very much indebted to Mr Muir, as I am myself, for first introducing them to Kafka's work. They may also feel some surprise that I have not made use of his very pleasing and sensitive version, but have preferred to use one of my own. This was not done out of any feeling that I could better it as a whole. Yet I have found that on many occasions the precise nuance which I wished to emphasize was not present in the English word chosen by Mr Muir to render the German. I have also found, though far less frequently, mistakes in the rendering of quite important passages. Where, therefore, there is a very wide divergence between my rendering and that of the definitive edition, as there is on about half-a-dozen occasions, I can only request that the German text be consulted.

R. D. G.

I

The temptation when reading Kafka is to ask what he is driving at, instead of looking at what he says. This may account for the number of interpretations of his work that have appeared, claiming to give an account of his symbolism that will explain the mysterious fascination he undoubtedly does exercise. Yet the reader of these interpretations is likely to feel as dissatisfied when he has finished as he was when he had only the works themselves to go on. He will probably agree with Angel Flores, editor of *The Kafka Problem*, that 'everyone who has read Kafka, not to mention many who haven't, seems not to have the slightest doubt that he understands him perfectly, and moreover that he is the only one who does'. There is, at all events, complete disagreement between the interpreters who see in Kafka's novels and stories primarily the account of a religious quest, and those, chiefly psycho-analysts and sociologists, who find the theological versions 'totally unsupported by internal evidence'. After some study of these conflicting views, one might well conclude that Kafka had left his meaning unclear, that he had nothing definite to communicate, and that a writer so vague and ambiguous was not worth long attention.

Any further attempt at interpretation can only add to the numbers on one side or the other. It can also do only damage to Kafka's reputation, for if his work is so esoteric that it requires special knowledge to clarify it—knowledge of the Kabbala, for instance, or of the sect of Chassidim, of Barthian theology or of Freudian symbolism—its literary value cannot be great. If Kafka is worth reading at all, as a literary artist, he must be accessible not to initiates merely, but to readers who have a serious concern for the depiction of actuality and who pay a scrupulous attention to the language in which it is depicted. To offer an interpretation of him, as though it were the unravelling of a secret, is to assert his lack of artistry.

To say this is to imply that the only satisfactory approach to Kafka must be not that of the theologian, the philosopher, or the psycho-analyst, but that of the literary critic. The ideal I have in mind is the one adumbrated by Dr F. R. Leavis, to whose published work I am glad to acknowledge my debt. 'The business of the literary critic is to attain a peculiar completeness of response and to observe a peculiarly strict relevance in developing his response into commentary; he must be on his guard against abstracting improperly from what is in front of him and against any premature or irrelevant generalizing—of it or from it. His first concern is to enter into possession of the given poem (let us say) in its concrete fullness, and his constant concern is never to lose his completeness of possession, but rather to increase it.'[1] Some writers on Kafka—Friedrich Beissner and Eliseo Valdes, to

[1] F. R. Leavis, *The Common Tradition* (London, 1953), p. 213.

2

mention two[1]—have already attempted something of this kind of approach, an approach which does not present a series of parallels drawn from non-literary sources, but is based on an examination of language, imagery, leitmotifs, the depiction of character and other purely literary considerations. The present study, concerning itself almost entirely with one novel, also keeps within the province of criticism. If it demonstrates, among other things, how one can 'assume too easily that a poet's essential "belief" is what can be most readily extracted as such from his works by a philosopher'[2] it will have been useful in one way. I hope it will also be useful in another. It does conclude—and when the conclusion is reached I don't think it will look like 'premature or irrelevant generalizing'—that *The Castle* is not the account of a featureless path leading nowhere, nor a satire, nor a 'trotzdem', an act of defiance, but the description of a metamorphosis of the kind attributed by Christians to the action of grace.

Putting this down now may give the impression of an only half-hearted allegiance to literary criticism. Certainly I am convinced that *The Castle* is important in its bearing on religion. But this is not the same thing as saying that it should be interpreted from a particular religious point of view. There is still a distinction between doing that and recording the response one has been enabled to bring to a work of art.

[1] Cf. Friedrich Beissner, *Der Erzähler Franz Kafka* (Stuttgart, 1952), and Eliseo Valdes, 'Kafka's Distorted Mask', *The Kenyon Review*, Winter 1948.
[2] F. R. Leavis, *op. cit.* p. 222.

The distinction I have in mind will be the clearer for a preliminary (though incomplete) account of the general state of Kafka studies at the moment. This will serve not only to show the variety of possibilities resulting from the interpretative method, but also to indicate where the fault of that method lies. At the same time it may justify the extensive treatment of a single work, which, I have claimed, is not worth reading if it cannot be understood by means of the equipment that civilized people are able to bring to it. I have tried to say nothing that is not common sense. Yet as Goethe observed, 'it would be a real benefit for mankind if one could demonstrate convincingly to common sense how far it can reach, which is as far as it ever needs to reach in earthly life'.[1]

I have indicated the general division of interpretative critics into a religious camp and an anti-religious one. There are, however, further divergences in each, and this is particularly noticeable in the religious group. All the representatives of this group are agreed that a religious quest is involved, but few agree about the nature of the quest. For Max Brod, the friend of Kafka and editor of his posthumous works, *The Trial* and *The Castle* present 'the twin appearance of the Godhead (in the sense of the Kabbala)—Justice and Grace'.[2] It is essentially a Jewish Kafka that Brod presents. On the other hand, some have insisted much

---

[1] Goethe, *Maximen und Reflexionen* (Jub. Ausg. IV, p. 249).
[2] Max Brod in *Das Schloss* (New York, 1946), p. 418.

more strongly than Brod does on the Christian element in Kafka's work. These depend chiefly on Kafka's avowed sympathy with the Christian theologian Kierkegaard; one of them, John Kelly, claims that Kafka unwittingly produced a parallel to the Christian existentialist theology of his contemporary Karl Barth, in which the influence of Kierkegaard is strong. But wide as the difference may be between Jewish and Christian interpretations, it looks slight in comparison with a larger divergence. Until recently there was general agreement within this group that the ultimate goal of Kafka's quest (or rather that of K., his protagonist) was good, that K.'s spiritual journey might be compared with that of Bunyan's Christian, even though its conclusion was so tragically different. Thus Brod speaks of 'a reminiscence (albeit a very distant one and as it were reduced to a minimum) of Goethe's lines from *Faust*—"Whoe'er aspires unweariedly Is not beyond redeeming"'. Similarly Albert Camus: '*Le Procès* diagnostique et *Le Château* imagine un traitement. Mais le remède proposé ici ne guérit pas. Il fait seulement rentrer la maladie dans la vie normale. Il aide à l'accepter. Dans un certain sens (pensons à Kierkegaard) il la fait chérir.'[1] This claims to find at least an element of positive affirmation in Kafka's work, as does the comment of Claude-Edmonde Magny: 'The cup must be drained to the lees, we must suffer without comprehending the inhuman sentence through which, like the condemned man in the *Penal Colony*, we attain the ecstasy of the

[1] Albert Camus, *Le Mythe de Sisyphe* (Paris, 1942), p. 180.

sixth hour.'[1] In both these quotations there is the picture of a man who endures suffering and hopes only for the release which death brings. But it is fundamentally a search for God in which the man is engaged: 'L'ultime tentative de l'arpenteur, c'est de retrouver Dieu à travers ce qui le nie.'[2] The tendency in the interpretation of Erich Heller is, however, in a different direction. Professor Heller is willing to admit that *The Castle*, which he makes his chief concern, has 'religious relevance', but, he adds, 'it is hard to see how *The Castle* can possibly be called a religious allegory with a pilgrim of the type of Bunyan's as its hero'. There is, he observes, no pilgrimage in this work, 'no motion, no change, no metamorphosis'. Neither Kafka nor K. makes any progress, and the total impression left by the book is the impossibility of ever making any. 'The castle of Kafka's novel is, as it were, the heavily fortified garrison of a company of Gnostic demons, successfully holding an advanced position against the manœuvres of an impatient soul. I do not know of any conceivable idea of divinity which could justify those interpreters who see in the castle the residence of "divine law and divine grace".'

In short, Erich Heller holds that while *The Castle* is *about* a religious quest, it is a quest deplorably mistaken in its whole attitude. The 'misapprehension' (of critics like Brod and Edwin Muir) 'would seem to reflect a very profound religious confusion, so

[1] C.-E. Magny, *The Kafka Problem*, ed. A. Flores (New York, 1946), p. 79.
[2] Albert Camus, *op. cit.* p. 183.

6

profound indeed that one can scarcely hold the
individual critic responsible for it. It is the very
spiritual uprootedness of the age which has deprived
us of all sureness of religious discrimination.'[1] This
comment marks a cleavage within the religious group
such as has not, I think, appeared before, at any rate
to the same extent. It comes close to the view of those
'naturalist' critics (to use Neider's term) who regard
the theological implications of Kafka's work as symp-
toms of disease, though it differs from them in believing
that a truer religious attitude than Kafka's is conceivable and desirable. The problem here, then,
seems to turn on the interpretation of an image or
symbol: spirit of health or goblin damn'd?—and on
whether K.'s struggle to reach the castle deserves
sympathy or not.

Within the 'naturalist' school this problem does
not exist because theological questions are regarded
as meaningless in any case. For Edwin Burgum Kafka
is certainly a religious man, and even a mystic, but
this is in his mouth the reverse of praise. Kafka, he
writes, 'like Kierkegaard, his favourite philosopher,
represents the breakdown of mysticism itself, both
as a discipline and as a philosophy. In the light
of the great religious mystics of history, to emphasize Kafka's religious mysticism can only mean to
share his own incapacity for reasoned judgment.'
Burgum emphasizes that Kafka's personality verged
upon the psychopathic, and anticipates that 'sooner

[1] Erich Heller, *The Disinherited Mind* (Cambridge, 1952), pp. 172, 173, 175, 160.

7

or later psychiatrists will discover that his novels are as rewarding an object of investigation as those of Dostoevsky'. The interest here, therefore, is not so much in what Kafka wrote, for its own sake, as in deciding how such hallucinations came to be written down, and how they responded to the 'similar anxiety in the Weimar Republic'. Burgum writes with scientific detachment: 'Whatever happens we accept without any emotional involvement of our own.' His approach is the perfectly justifiable sociological one and his finding is that, 'stated in political terms, [Kafka's] dilemma was that he could not become a fascist . . . He was forced to wander into death and madness alone. For Hitler had not yet offered the fantasy of a fantasy in his confraternity of the doomed, who for the time being were able to distort their gloom into the hallucination of a glory. We who are more happily situated than Kafka can draw from his novels the desolate pleasure that there too we should have gone if we had been unable to believe in the potentialities of democracy and the common man.'[1] This conclusion appears to be a natural consequence of the author's atheistic standpoint. Once the existence of God is denied, all desire to attain authority or submit to it tends to be seen in terms of the State. Translated into political terms the utterances of theologians may seem to have a totalitarian ring. Yet Burgum might offer the plausible retort that Kafka does in fact write in terms of a

[1] Edwin Burgum, *The Kafka Problem*, ed. A. Flores, pp. 299, 302, 302, 315, 305, 317.

8

bureaucracy, and that the name of God probably does not occur anywhere in his work. There can be no demonstrable proof that Kafka was not concerned with political and social questions.

There is, however, a cleavage also within the 'naturalist' school. For while Burgum regards Kafka as a mystic who unwittingly revealed the disastrous nature of his beliefs, Charles Neider sees him as a deliberate satirist. 'Kafka's works', he claims, 'are attacks on cabalas', by which he means 'the mystical school—by far the greatest cabala of them all', and in general all religious and transcendental interpreters of things. Kafka was a writer who could not under any circumstances allow himself any irrationality, any irrational form of acceptance, and who therefore found himself trapped within the limitations of reason. He escaped from this trap, in so far as he did escape at all, not by continuing his religious quest further and further, but by examining the quest in an objective fashion. The result of this, in Neider's view, is a satire on irrationalism—'a satire on cabalism permeates *The Castle*'; Kafka's portrayal of cabalism is 'an ironic and implied comment on it'; 'Kafka's fable in *The Trial* as well as in the rest of his work is the education of all youthful idealists into adjusted middle-aged "realists".' With this attitude to the work as a whole, Neider proceeds to a mainly psycho-analytical account of the individual pieces, demonstrating the conscious exploitation of Freudian symbols. Thus: 'A castle, like a village, town, citadel, and fortress, is a symbol of a woman and a mother. A

9

count is a father-symbol, like emperor, king and presi-
dent. The count's permission is necessary for K. to enter
the Castle; i.e. the father's permission is necessary
for the son to possess his mother incestuously.'[1]

This, like the application of Burgum's atheism, is
a consistent use of Freudian psychology. But it does
not provide the basis for a consistent account of the
novel. It does not explain why K., who is in a village
and comes from a town—both mother-symbols on
this interpretation—should want to enter a castle. Nor
does it explain why K.'s aim is not to possess a woman
but to meet a male official 'face to face'. No doubt
further psychological reasons could be found to
account for these difficulties. But there is a graver
objection than this, quite apart from the fact that
Kafka, in his religious 'Meditations', described psycho-
analysis as a 'helpless error'.[2] Neider's criticism of
theological interpretations is that they are 'totally
unsupported by internal evidence'. That is, there is
nowhere any explicit reference to theological concepts.
On the other hand there is no explicit reference to
Freudian concepts either. To equate the castle with
a mother-symbol is as arbitrary an act as to equate it
with the divinity. The interpretation depends in both
cases on the personal attitude of the interpreter rather
than on any direct warrant from the text.

Four pictures of Kafka have thus emerged so far:
the tragically enduring seeker after truth; the mistaken

[1] Charles Neider, *Kafka: His Mind and Art* (London, 1949), pp. 152, 10, 37,
38, 37, 124.
[2] Kafka, *Tagebücher und Briefe* (Prague, 1937), p. 219.

upholder of a false religious attitude; the unwitting revealer of the folly of all forms of mysticism; and the conscious satirist of such beliefs. The interpreters have only one thing in common: the determination to derive some positive belief from Kafka's work, if only by reaction from it. In this they illustrate the saying of Kafka's in his 'Reflections on Sin and Suffering': 'Man cannot live without a permanent trust in something indestructible in himself, although both the indestructible element and the trust may remain permanently hidden from him.'[1] . . . On this point at least Kafka and his critics agree. The difficulties arise from trying to decide whether Kafka himself had such a belief, whether he was conscious of it, whether it remained unconscious all his life, whether he regarded it with scepticism, irony, or deep seriousness.

These are questions that cannot be answered so long as there is any possibility of the critic's having read some of his own, or some of a commonly accepted form of belief into Kafka's work. And the risk of such a bias is present in all interpretations which begin by asking what the castle, or any other image in the stories and novels, stands for. What tends to happen, to judge by my own experience, is this. One observes certain parallels between some features of the narrative and a quite distinct, though possibly related system of beliefs, or exposition of doctrine, or an entirely personal experience of one's own. This is often useful and serves to illuminate the passage in a

[1] Kafka, *Tagebücher*, ed. cit. p. 205.

quite fresh way. Then comes the temptation to extend the parallelism so as to bring further aspects from each side of the equation into relationship. Thus a great deal of time can be spent in drawing parallels between, say, Kierkegaardian theology and concepts derived from Kafka. But there is always the feeling, accompanying the effort, that one is erecting a scaffolding round the meaning of the work itself, and later on comes the realization that the parallels have served subtly to distract one's attention from the text in hand. To establish the case one has tinkered a little here, not allowed for a nuance there, accepted a general similarity for a detailed one. Neither one half of the equation nor the other is really elucidated by this means: each has interfered with the other and has obstructed fuller realization. An unbiased view can only be achieved, or only be approached, if all such parallels are steadily excluded. In the final analysis, that is, when the analysis is complete, interpretation is an inescapable obligation. But the novel must first be experienced as purely as possible in its own terms.

The point about *The Castle* is that, read on its own terms, it gives no direct support either to a theological or to a psycho-analytical interpretation. Both groups of critics run the risk of supposing that Kafka was writing in terms of allegory, that is, that he originally thought in terms of theology or of psycho-analysis and then translated these terms into the language of his novel, so that the critic's task is to reverse the work of interpretation and lay bare what Kafka originally had in mind. As though Kafka were a priest or a psychologist who mistook his vocation. This attitude ignores the possibility that Kafka worked as a literary artist, not inventing complex equivalents for a system of beliefs already held, but exploring the possibilities of an image which presented itself to his imagination, in this case the image of a castle and of a man trying to reach it. The ramified account of such an image has to remain consistent with itself, but not, as a primary requirement, with such conceptions as other people's ideas on the nature of God, or on the influence of childhood experience on religious belief. The task of a literary critic is to explore that account and consider such questions as unity, consistency, coherence, and in so far as he is thinking in literary terms, his task stops when he has described his experience of the work fully. He is not called upon in his capacity as a literary critic to decide between the claims of rival schools of religious thought. At the same time, he is not required to suspend judgment indefinitely on this vital matter.

So this is the method adopted in the present study. It attempts to say what the castle means, not to the writer, but to the people in the novel; to ask not what things stand for but what they do and how they function; to remain on the surface of the novel and not to probe for what might lie beyond. The probing can wait. 'There is indeed the inexpressible. This *shows* itself; it is the mystical.'[1]

---

[1] Ludwig Wittgenstein, *Tractatus Logico-Philosophicus* (London, 1922), para. 6.522.

II

'While I was beseeching Our Lord today that He would speak through me, since I could find nothing to say and had no idea how to begin to carry out the obligation laid upon me by obedience, a thought occurred to me which I will now set down, in order to have some foundation on which to build. I began to think of the soul as if it were a castle made of a single diamond or of very clear crystal, in which there are many rooms, just as in Heaven there are many mansions.'[1]

I quote these words from the opening page of one of the most famous works of mysticism, St Teresa's *Interior Castle*, not in order to point out any similarity with Kafka's work but to illustrate a difference. There are, I should say, many similarities, but to explore them would distract attention both from St Teresa and from Kafka. To observe the difference between them will, however, bring out an essential quality of Kafka's work. St Teresa begins by thinking of the soul and goes on to find an equivalent for it. She is quite explicit: 'I began to think of the soul as if it were a castle'—and there is no possible doubt about her meaning. The result is that while her work has little 'poetic' effect, that is, it does not stir the imagin-

---

[1] St Teresa, *Complete Works*, trans. E. Allison Peers (London, 1946), vol. 2, p. 202.

ation as Kafka's does, she gives a clear picture of the progression towards the innermost mansion of her castle, and is able to affirm that, when this stage is reached 'as far as one can understand, the soul (I mean the spirit of this soul) is made one with God'.[1] Her meaning is clear, then, until one asks by what right she makes this affirmation, and what she means by 'soul'. To the first question she replies with the proviso 'as far as one can understand'. With the second she is not concerned. All we know, from this work, of her conception of 'soul' is what she tells us about this castle. Thus, to say that her castle symbolizes the soul is not to provide information about what the soul 'really' is. One accepts the equation in order to enlarge one's notion of what the soul meant to St Teresa.

This will serve to illustrate a definition of allegorical method. In allegory an equivalence is established between a real object or event and a word expressing some abstract quality or metaphysical concept. In this way Bunyan speaks of the Slough of Despond, Doubting Castle, and Vanity Fair. The goal of his Christian is a City which is explicitly called heaven. But in calling it so Bunyan is dependent on a word, and words are not realities but conventions defined by function and use. Bunyan does not establish any identity between his City and any transcendent reality such as heaven. He implies that when he says 'heaven' he thinks of a city paved with gold and with angels pouring out praise and thanksgiving. This is what

[1] St Teresa, *Complete Works*, vol. II, p. 335.

15

the word 'heaven' means to him. But he does not show or even imply that heaven is so. He does not reach out into a transcendental world by means of his allegory, any more than St Teresa does. Rather, he gives a noble extension to the meaning of the word as it is normally used. All is dependent on the saving clause 'as far as one can understand'.

Kafka's method is different. He studiously avoids equivalents, while at the same time suggesting by an unusual emphasis here or there that more is implied than one is at first aware of. He has in fact a literary artist's distrust of words to express his meaning, since words are conventions that settle into rigidity with use, forming a world of their own separate from the reality they are supposed to represent. Anything which distracts attention from the immediate object in view is to be eschewed. To describe one object in terms of another, perhaps the most common device in literature, seems to him like failure. Metaphors, he wrote in his diary, were one of the many things which made him despair about writing. Thus Kafka will never offer the description of a real object or event and then say, 'Of course I really mean so-and-so.' If he were to do so, the reader would at once be satisfied: 'Oh yes—that—of course, I know what that means.' Or he would tend to have such a feeling, and the precise nature of the reality with which Kafka was presenting him would escape attention. Accordingly, there are many minute descriptions but very few abstract words to sum them up. Kafka always remains dependent on words, but he does what he can to strip them of conventionality.

Here is an example of this aspect of Kafka's method from the first chapter of *The Castle*. K. has just abandoned his first attempt to reach the castle on foot, and turns aside into a house where he is accorded on the whole a friendly reception. Among all the activity going on there, his attention is drawn particularly to a young woman who sits throughout motionless in a corner; indeed so strong is the impression she makes on him that as he is finally about to leave he actually jumps round in order to face her once again. This dominant figure in the scene is described in these terms:

'But more surprising still, although one could not say just what was surprising about it, was the corner on the right. From a great gap, the only one in the back wall of the room, there shone down a pale, snowy light, probably from the courtyard, giving the dress of a woman wearily almost lying in a high-backed chair far back in the corner a gleam as though of silk. She had a baby at her breast. Around her played a few children, peasant children obviously; but she seemed not to belong to them. Of course illness and weariness make even peasants look refined'. [A little later] . . . the woman in the chair lay as though lifeless, not even looking down at the child at her breast, but gazing vaguely aloft. K. must have looked long at this unchanging, lovely, sorrowful picture, but then he must have fallen asleep . . . [And finally] To everyone's surprise K. fairly leapt so as to turn about and stand before the woman. With weary blue eyes she looked at K., a silken transparent kerchief spread down to the middle of her forehead, the baby was sleeping at her breast. "Who are you?" asked K. Disdainfully—it was not clear whether the contempt was meant for K. or for her own reply—she said, "A girl from the castle"' (pp. 22-4).[1]

Kafka heightens attention by observing that the whole scene is in some undefined way surprising. The reader is set wondering. At the end, if one wants to describe this part of the scene in a few words, one is tempted to say that this is a sort of nativity scene with the Virgin Mary. So much does correspond with paintings of this kind: the gap in the wall (not a window but one of those tumbledown openings favoured by nativity painters), the suggestion of snow and of silken garments, the suckling child, and the unusual headwear in this village so modern as to be equipped with telephones. But you are in doubt. Nowhere is it said that this is a picture of a girl who resembles the Virgin Mary. Why is she almost lying down? Why does she not look at the child? Why does she speak with contempt? If there is any symbolical intent, what does this meeting signify? The suggestive overtones tempt one to extend the parallel beyond justifiable limits. As soon as any equivalence is asserted it needs to be withdrawn. It is left to the reader to discover for himself wherein the surprise lay.

[1] References to *The Castle* are paginated as in the third edition of *Das Schloss* (New York, 1946). They correspond, in the early chapters, exactly with the pagination of the English definitive edition, but in the latter the text (excluding appendices) covers 25 more pages. An increasingly large adjustment is necessary to find references in the English edition.

Leaving it to the reader is also a part of Kafka's method. One common feature of his work is what may be called the 'Vexierbild' technique, the name deriving from those pictures, originally so popular in the seventeenth century, where a given set of lines and shading can be interpreted in two entirely different ways, according to the way in which they are sized up by the eye. The same idea is employed today in those psychological tests where the subject is presented with a picture representing equally well the face of an old hag or the figure of a luscious blonde. Neither interpretation is *the* correct one, both are possible. The messages received by K. from the castle are ambiguous in this way: they appear in the main hostile, as K. interprets them, but he is aware that they are not necessarily so. As the narrator of the novel puts it: 'These were undoubtedly contradictions, they were so visible that they must be intended. The crazy idea, in regard to such an authority as this, that indecision might have played any part in producing them, scarcely occurred to K. He saw in them rather an open choice presented to him; it was left to him to make what he wanted of the orders in the letter' (p. 36). The letter, like everything else connected with the castle, can be interpreted favourably, with good will. Not only K., but also the reader, is faced with this choice.

Perhaps the clearest example of this technique occurs in the story *A Country Doctor*. This is the account of a doctor who is called out in the middle of the night to attend a boy with a gruesome wound in his side. When he arrives, the doctor is able to afford no more comfort to the boy than to say, 'That's how it is' ('Es ist wirklich so'). The wound exists and there is nothing more to be done about it. The description of the wound, however, is not by any means straightforward. It is carefully, ingeniously constructed so as to suggest at the same time a flower:

'In his right side, near the hip, a wound has opened up, as big as the palm of your hand. Rose ['Rosa', literally 'pink', but suggesting both the German 'Rose' and the name of a character in the story], in many tints, dark in the deepest parts, growing lighter towards the edges, finely grained, the blood suffusing it in blotches, as open as the entrance to a mine. Thus it looks from a distance. From close at hand a further complication appears. Who can set eyes on it without whistling under his breath? Worms, as thick as my little finger, rosy with their own, and spattered with other blood, are twisting their white little heads and numerous small legs towards the light, held fast in the depths of the wound. Poor lad, there is no help for you. I have found out your great wound; this flower in your side will destroy you.'

The reality with which the doctor seeks to comfort the boy is in fact ambiguous, though neither of them is conscious of it. Almost every detail will fit both the rose and the wound, so that there is a kind of challenge to the reader, if one wishes, to see beauty in this abominable ugliness, recalling Camus' definition of K.'s aim, 'de retrouver Dieu à travers ce qui le nie, de le reconnaître, non selon nos catégories de bonté et de beauté, mais derrière les visages vides et hideux de son indifférence, de son injustice, et de sa haine'.[1] Yet the passage is not successful. It is ingenious rather than compelling, and a re-reading suggests that no such wound ever existed, that Kafka never could have seen one like it. It seems more probable that what he saw first was a rose, which suggested to him a wound: the beauty first became ugly in *his* mind, and thus the detailed parallels appear contrived. The image illustrates only Kafka's inability, at this stage in his life (*A Country Doctor* was written in 1916) to see things except in ambiguous terms. Oppressed with suffering, with a world war raging round him, he concludes this story with the picture of the doctor, 'naked, exposed to the frost of this most wretched era, with an earthly carriage and unearthly horses, an old man wandering to and fro'. It must have been the inadequacy of this tortuous dichotomy which made Kafka write the words in his diary, quoted by Max Brod on the fly-leaf of his biography. 'Pieces like *A Country Doctor* can still give me a temporary satisfaction . . . . But I shall be happy only if I ever manage to lift up the world into the pure, the true, the unchangeable.' Kafka employs the technique of dual description, though rarely in so blatant a form as this, because it fits the mood he is in, swaying between earth and heaven. But his ultimate aim is to set out the one image which admits of no contradiction, paradox or uncertainty.

Another of the 'terrible' stories, *In the Penal Colony*

[1] Albert Camus, *op. cit.* p. 183.

(written even earlier, in 1914), depicts a similarly ghastly situation, in which once again the barest possibility of a happier view is present. Here almost all depends on the interpretation of a genitive. The narrative is mainly concerned with an instrument of torture and execution, under which prisoners are placed so that they may realize the exact nature of their guilt. Those who do suffer in this way are rewarded at the end of the sixth hour: their faces are transfigured, and they meet their inevitable end in the possession of truth. At length, the officer who has been in control of these operations is persuaded to lay himself on the machine. At once, miraculously and without any human intervention, the machine sets in motion as it were of its own accord. But the officer (who, it is just barely suggested, is a sacrificial figure) far from being transfigured, remains transfixed on the machine with a spike through his forehead. The machine can never be used again, since it has broken in pieces under the strain, and this much at least has been accomplished by the officer's inter-vention. No one can suffer again under the inexorable law which governed it, although, as usually happens in Kafka's work, no one in the story realizes this or draws attention to the fact. Yet the dominant picture at the end of the story is that of the officer, unrewarded and untransfigured, an image of pointless suffering. Humane feeling is revolted at the apparent suggestion that all this torture has been a cruel farce. Yet once again there is just the possibility of an alternative interpretation. In describing the appearance of the

officer's face after his death the narrator emphasizes
that there was 'no sign of the promised redemption',
such as had come, at least temporarily, to the earlier
sufferers under the machine. He adds, however, and
here ambiguity enters, that the face had 'the expression
of life', 'den Ausdruck des Lebens'. This may be
taken to mean that the officer's face remained as it
was during his life, unaltered by experience, and it
is taken solely in that sense by, for example, Herbert
Tauber.[1] But it may also mean that absurdly, with a
spike through the forehead, the face had the look of
life about it, that this image of total destruction is
also the sign of resurrection. Read along these lines,
the details of the story assume a fresh and more
positive significance. The fact that the officer, the
controller of the machine, by his voluntary death
preserves all future generations from similar suffering,
together with the possibility that he lives again after
his frightful execution, is illuminated by reference to
Pauline theology. 'Christ hath redeemed us from the
curse of the law, being made a curse for us: for it is
written, Cursed is every one that hangeth on a tree'
(Galatians, iii. 13). Not that the officer bears any
resemblance to Christ, except in the manner of his
death and its consequences. To press the parallel is
to lose the thread of Kafka's story, and to imagine it
far more positive than in fact it is. There is no open
declaration of faith here, as there is in St Paul. On the
contrary, ambiguity is the keynote. The interpretation

---

[1] G. C. H. Tauber, *Franz Kafka, Eine Deutung seiner Werke*, (Zürich and
New York, 1941), p. 65.

which sees the officer suitably rewarded for his inhumanity, and which, faced with the problem of
suffering, ends with a savage nihilism, is still justifiable.
The text will bear that interpretation and even invites
it. On the other hand, buried in that genitive, 'the
expression of life', and in one or two other details of
the story too complex to be examined except at great
length, there remains the bare hint of a triumphant
solution. This much at least can be said for the story,
that by leaving interpretation open it forces on the
reader a fuller realization of the implications involved
in both views. But the emphasis lies mainly on the
nihilistic view. The mood is still that of the country
doctor–'That's how it is'; no single view of 'the pure,
the true and unchangeable' is presented. Once again
an entry from Kafka's diary provides an implied
comment, with imagery not far removed from that of
the iron spike in the *Penal Colony:* 'A heavy downpour
of rain. Meet the rain, let the iron rays penetrate you,
glide along in the water that is sweeping you away,
but stay like that, and wait, erect, till the sun comes
streaming suddenly, endlessly in.'[1] The *Penal Colony*
is too immersed in suffering to be unambiguous.

The Castle is of course shot through with ambiguities too, as is evident in the very form of narration.
It was begun, according to Max Brod, as a novel in
the first person, and only after the opening chapters
had been written was the pronoun 'I' replaced by the
initial 'K.'. This gives rise to a curious effect. Almost

[1] Quoted by Max Brod on the fly-leaf of *Franz Kafka, eine Biographie* (New
York, 1946).

24

nothing is related except what is actually experienced by K. A passage of conversation in which the villagers poke fun at K. behind his back is excluded, and appears only in the deleted fragments. Because of this the reader soon grows accustomed to seeing everything from K.'s point of view. On the other hand it is not K. who tells the story, but, as the literary convention has it, the narrator, who does not necessarily represent either K.'s or Kafka's view. The narrator tells the story in the past tense, like one who already knows what the outcome is to be, and once or twice he does reveal his foreknowledge, as when he writes: 'K., on the other hand, was fighting for something vitally close, for himself; and moreover, *at least at the very outset,* he was fighting by his own will, for he was the attacker' (p. 73). The narrator overlooks the scene and suggests that, as he is aware, there came a time, not yet reached in the narrative, when K. was assisted in his fight by some will other than his own. (There are, he says later, 'other forces' fighting on K.'s behalf.) And so throughout, while there is almost a compulsion on the reader to experience the events of the novel as K. experiences them, one is aware of a suggested overall scheme into which these experiences may fit, of an invitation to see the experiences from other points of view than K.'s. There is a mingling of objective narrative–the narrator telling the reader what went on, and subjective reaction–the limitation of all interpretation to what went on in K.'s mind. Rarely has any author observed the implications of the use of a narrator more stringently than Kafka does

25

in this novel. The result of this, however, is to provide, amid all the ambiguity and paradox which appears, one shred of complete certainty. There can never be any doubt as to what is in K.'s mind, for the narrator has, by convention, accurate insight into it. In this consideration lies the germ of the idea by which Kafka was able, towards the end of *The Castle*, to present that single-minded view to which the entries in his diary refer.

III

From the opening chapter of *The Castle* onwards, the note of ambiguity is struck. When K. first arrives, the castle does not even seem to exist: 'not even the faintest gleam was there to hint of the great castle', and he stands on the bridge gazing up at 'the apparent void' (p. 11). Only later does this empty nothingness become a reality. In the same way, K. at once affects, on his arrival at the inn, to have no inkling of the castle's presence, though it soon becomes obvious that he has come because of a summons from the owner of the castle himself. His reception at the inn is equally baffling: in quick succession he is told, first that no one at the castle has ever heard of him, then that the head clerk has telephoned personally to say he is expected. Next morning, he is confronted once more with a shifting outline which appears now negative, now positive. On the wall of the taproom he sees a dark portrait in a dark frame: 'Even from his palliasse he had noticed it, but had not been able to distinguish the details from a distance, and had thought the actual picture had been taken from the frame, so that only the black backing was to be seen' (p. 17). But it turns out once again that the apparent void is filled. On closer inspection K. sees that the frame contains a portrait—of a high official, as he learns from the landlord. Thus the reader is brought from the outset into a world where presence and absence, affirmation and denial, recognition and bafflement follow rapidly on one another. Something akin to the 'Vexierbild' technique is being frequently exploited.

The same contradictoriness characterizes almost everything else that is ever related of the castle, making critical statements a highly complex matter. Nevertheless, it is possible to describe, not what the castle stands for, but what it means to the villagers and to K., in indisputable terms. First, as to the villagers. One of the first things K. learns from them is that there is 'no distinction' between the castle and the village: 'anyone who lives or lodges here, to a certain extent lives or lodges in the castle' (p. 11). Again, when K. complains that he belongs neither with the villagers nor to the castle, he is told, 'There is no difference between the villagers and the castle' (p. 20). K.'s mistress, Frieda, even claims that the highest official ever referred to, Klamm, is visible in the face of such minor personages as K.'s assistants: 'Their eyes, those simple yet sparkling eyes, remind me somehow of the eyes of Klamm; yes, that's it, it's Klamm's look that sometimes pierces through me out of their eyes' (p. 166). K's retort to this, 'you see Klamm everywhere', might be taken ambiguously, like all these statements. All of them could, just conceivably, be made by everyday villagers about an everyday castle, or about an official residing there. At the same time there is the suggestion, which smacks more of theological ideas, that the castle is immanent in the village, and Klamm immanent in the inhabitants, in much the same way that God is said to be immanent in the world. With most authors other than Kafka the equivalence would be more or less taken for granted, though in his case it is necessary to proceed more carefully. Nevertheless there are many more suggestions of this kind. For the villagers, whatever is done by the castle is right. It moves in a mysterious way, not always intelligible to them, but it never makes a mistake. Its officials are, they assert, full of loving-kindness, always ready to sacrifice themselves, though they also know how to chastise when need arises. Klamm in particular is the idol of the villagers. When the course of events mystifies them they find comfort in the reflection that 'it is the will of Klamm'. To be Klamm's beloved is the highest distinction that the women among them can reach, although when K. speaks of meeting Klamm 'face to face' they are horrified. Some of these attributed qualities can refer to the ordinary relationship of citizens with a bureaucracy; some of them could refer, if a psychoanalytical vocabulary is used, to the complexities of a father-relationship. But neither of these interpretations accounts for the totality of the qualities. If Klamm is a father he is a father not merely to K. but to the whole village. If he is an official he has the strange power of transmitting his piercing glance to his servants. Infallibility, immanence, love, inscrutability, wrath, inaccessibility, these contradictory qualities are the ones commonly ascribed to the divinity. Significantly, however, the villagers never use any such word. And one is not entitled without more ado, given the complexities of this novel, to say that that is what they really mean. The most that can be affirmed at this stage is that the villagers speak of Klamm and the castle in the terms they would presumably use in speaking of God. This is not to allegorize the novel: it is not to suggest that, as in allegory, the equivalence is readily establishable. It is rather to define the nature of the castle as it appears to the villagers. We are still so to speak in the realm of opinion, the opinion of certain characters in a work of fiction.

Indeed, as the villagers announce their convictions about the nature of the castle and its officials, both K. and the reader grow suspicious. It is too often apparent that the villagers are over-anxious to demonstrate the absolute rightness of the castle's ways. It does not strike them as odd that the castle is unattainable and yet somehow in the village, or that, while some of them claim to have been Klamm's beloved, it is unthinkable that anyone should meet him face to face. They either skate away over these paradoxes, or consider them unimportant. The sceptical frame of mind must interpret this as humbug or credulity. Although scarcely any of the villagers have been in the castle (and the one who has, Barnabas, is the least certain of all) almost every one has his cut-and-dried version of what goes on there. Secretly, however, and perhaps unknown to themselves, they seem to hate and fear it. Some part of them knows that they are ignorant, that they have no means of telling what the castle is like from the inside, and they desperately conceal this ignorance from their surface selves. They save face by the partial concession, the half-admission, the ambiguous word that seems to say the right thing while allowing doubt to emerge to a scarcely perceptible degree. They betray themselves by their gestures and expressions, by their unnoticed self-contradictions, by the sudden and uncontrolled outbursts of savagery in their language, which belie their professions of charitable concern for K. This is particularly true of the village elder ('der Gemeinde-vorsteher'),[1] who sets out to instruct K. in the castle's ways and who speaks 'with a self-contented smile, as though everything depended on his orders, although nobody was able so much as to suspect the fact' (p. 78). (That, at least, is how K. interprets his expression.) When K. puts a question to him which demands real knowledge of the castle he is strangely silent:

'"She is beautiful", said K. [of the virgin-like girl previously met], "but a little pale and sickly. She comes from the castle, I daresay?" He said this half as a question. The elder looked at the clock, poured medicine into a spoon, and hastily swallowed it. "I suppose you only know the office arrangements in the castle?" K. asked rudely. "Yes", said the elder, with an ironical and yet grateful smile. "And they're the most important"' (p. 84).

The elder is glad to accept K.'s proffered escape-

---

[1] Referred to in the earlier English translation as 'the Superintendent', in the most recent as 'the Mayor'. Both titles imply too high a position.

hole and to make the most of it. (Though once again a less hostile interpretation might be placed on his words—he may be withholding information which would not profit K. at this stage.) The case is similar when he attempts to defend the castle's reputation for infallibility. He will never admit that any errors are made by officials, preferring to speak of 'so-called mistakes', with the result that his evasiveness becomes comic. Since no mistakes are made, K. inquires whether there are any officials appointed to investigate the mere possibility of error:

'"You are very strict", said the elder. "But multiply your strictness a thousandfold, and it will still be nothing compared with the strictness that the authorities apply to themselves. Only a complete stranger could put your question. Are there inspectors, you ask? There's nothing else but inspectors. Of course, they aren't there to find mistakes in the vulgar, literal sense, because mistakes don't occur, and even if a mistake does occur, as in your case, who is to say in the final analysis that it is a mistake"' (p. 81).

This hocus-pocus reads very much like a satire on some work of metaphysics or theology. The rugged determination to believe *quia impossibile est* can go no further than that. But the elder's words are only a sample of what K. hears on all sides. The villagers are so overshadowed by traditional, hearsay concepts of what the castle must be like, that they are unable to think for themselves. Sincerity and honesty of belief are immensely difficult so long as each accepts against his better judgment and at the same time has the conviction of being absolutely right. The castle, together with Klamm, is precisely their idol because they will neither attempt to penetrate its mysteries nor allow their inward self to protest at its contradictions. This does not conflict with the statement [1] previously made, that the villagers speak of the castle in the terms they would presumably use in speaking of God. But it does suggest that the image of the castle is not a straightforward representation of something other than itself. Rather, the castle is presented to the reader in a number of different aspects, shifting its meaning according to the point of view of the beholder. The aspect revealed in the account of the village elder seems to have been introduced with a mainly satirical intent.

Reverence for and blind faith in the castle's mysteries are not the only attitudes represented among the villagers. There is also the taciturn hostility of Amalia: 'I have not been initiated, and nothing could persuade me to be initiated.' There is the infinite scepticism of Barnabas, who, although he has access to the castle offices can never believe that this has any significance. There is the scholarly prudishness of the schoolmaster who begs K., in French, not to mention the ruler of the castle in the presence of innocent children. Whether these aspects are factual reports on people's reactions to the castle, whether they can be read as satirical, apologetic, condemnatory, or compassionate, is largely a matter of the reader's mood at any given moment. The intention of the narrator, and the inner minds of the characters, present as inscrutable a surface to the reader as does the castle itself.

The situation is different with K., however. Since everything is told from his point of view the reader has, by convention, accurate insight into K.'s mind. A definition of the castle as it appears to K. has, accordingly, particular interest. In contrast to the villagers, K. approaches the castle in complete ignorance, except for one article of faith. He knows that he has never been in the castle, and thinks it likely he will never get there, though he goes on trying almost to the end. (In the last few chapters that is no longer his concern.) He is, as the villagers frequently remind him, 'der Unwissendste', the least knowledgeable of all, and he accepts the title: 'It's true, I am ignorant ['unwissend', literally 'unknowing'–the German includes both meanings], but at any rate truth exists, and that's a very sad thing for me. But it has the advantage too that an ignorant man will dare more, and that's why I mean to bear ignorance gladly, and the bad consequences it must have, at least for a while and as long as strength lasts' (p. 72). The one certainty K. has is that truth exists–if only as a corollary to his own ignorance. He could not believe himself to be ignorant unless he believed in truth.

For K., the castle is not a symbol of truth but the only place he knows of where the truth might be ascertained; truth, that is, in an absolute sense, beyond any question of subjective opining. This gives a philosophical, metaphysical bent to his quest, for all that it is described in practical terms. Where the villagers spoke of the castle as though it were divine, K. speaks of it as though it held the truth. Once more, the two attitudes do not conflict; K.'s attitude, however, leads him into odd ambiguities, as irreconcilable as those of the villagers. On the one hand, he is searching desperately after truth of a kind which would give absolute certainty. On the other hand, he regards all claims to absolute certainty, as they are expressed by the villagers, with the utmost suspicion—he prefers to remain 'unknowing'. Thus at one moment the castle is his goal, because it contains the truth, at another it is his enemy, because it will make of him just such a presumptuous claimant to knowledge as the villagers are. K. himself recognizes this dual quality when he thinks of 'the greatness of his enemy and goal' (p. 57). And he fears the ful-filment of his aim like a threat (p. 27).

Similarly the castle appears to K. as a place of freedom—'up on the hill everything stood out freely and easily, or at least so it seemed from here' (p. 18). Truth and freedom are supposed to go hand in hand, and it is freedom from self-deception that K. is seeking. For all that, the castle also appears to him as an authority bent on compelling him to its own single view of things. He fears 'the power of his dispiriting surroundings, the habituation to disappointments, the power of the unnoticed influences of every moment' (p. 37) that are insidiously undermining his determi-nation to remain free of all presumptions of absolute certainty. There is no end to the infinite possibilities of interpreting each event, and it is the unknowing man who is most aware of this—'dem Unwissenden scheint alles möglich' (p. 72). To remain in this awareness is to be 'free', as K. now uses the word—to be untrammelled by custom and tradition, seeing innocently and freshly. So that for all that the castle is a place of freedom, it threatens freedom as K. requires it, and for this reason he takes up the struggle against it: 'I fear that life in the castle would not appeal to me. I want to be always free' (p. 16).

In one respect, then, K. is like a positivist confronting the castle with his earthly person, with his physical, not metaphysical standards. 'He had believed himself able to depend on his body, and without that conviction would never have set out on his path . . .' (p. 314). Or, to quote a particularly unambiguous, and perhaps for that reason deleted fragment, K. relies on his immovable 'irdische Schwere'—his earthly weight, to compel the castle into action on his behalf (p. 371). Yet while he preserves his freedom against the absolutism of authority, it is at the same time a quest for the unattainable that he is engaged in. If he did not want to know authority he would not go on with his attempts to enter the castle or to meet Klamm face to face. K. begins now to look as paradoxical as the villagers themselves. He differs from them only in that he continues to hold the twin aspects of the paradox apart, refusing to yield his rational right to investigate and criticize, and refusing to gloss over difficulties.

The castle is, for K., not merely the place where

truth and freedom seem to reside, it is also the place
that can tell him what kind of man he is. His efforts
to enter the place, at least in the earlier chapters,
spring from his need to have external confirmation
that he is what he takes himself to be. Unlike the
villagers, and, for that matter, unlike most human
beings, K. has considerable doubts on this subject.
He is, it is true, conscious of having been called into
the village to take up a job as land-surveyor. But now
that he is there, he doubts whether the summons was
genuine, can see no meaning or usefulness in his
profession, and thus needs the certainty which, he
thinks, only the castle can provide. Accordingly, his
first effort is to obtain from the officials some confirmation of the summons.

K.'s introspection here may be compared with that
of the tramway passenger in one of Kafka's earliest
stories, *Der Fahrgast*, who has similar doubts about
the propriety of his own existence. 'I cannot defend
at all', this passenger observes to himself, 'my standing
on this platform, holding on to this strap, letting
myself be carried along by this tram . . . Nobody
expects it of me, but that doesn't matter.' A girl stands
on the step beside him, waiting to alight, and her
complete lack of self-consciousness invites his detailed
observation. 'How is it', he asks, 'that she is not
surprised at herself, that she keeps her mouth closed
and says nothing of that kind at all?' This capacity
in the passenger for amazement at the sheer existence
of things and people is shared by K. In effect K. asks
such questions as 'Can my existence be justified?' 'Am I

the self I think I am?' 'Have I found and known myself?'
He would have been happier if he had left his hands
off this fruit of the tree of knowledge, but having once
become self-conscious enough to put the question he
has to go on with it.

Yet K. never puts the question as it is formulated
in his mind. When he has the chance to telephone
directly to the castle, instead of asking for confirmation
of his vocation he puts a question meant to deceive.
In spite of his attempt at sincerity there is some
compulsion in him to outwit rather than inquire. As a
result he pretends to be not himself but one of his assistants, and the form of his question is 'When can my
master come into the castle?' The answer he receives—
'Never'—may be taken as corresponding to his own
dishonesty. It does not say that K. will never enter the
castle, though it may imply that he will never do so
while he keeps up his pretence. In the same way, K.'s
other question, which he did mean to ask—'Who am I
then?'—receives the answer, 'You are the old assistant'
(p. 33). The castle is a mirror reflecting back to K.
the statements which he himself makes, for 'the old
assistant' is just what K. has claimed to be. If K. is
insincere the castle reflects it; whatever qualities he
shows will presumably also be similarly reflected.
At present K. is dissatisfied with this answer—he
demands some authoritative confirmation quite apart
from his own self. He is just as dissatisfied later,
when he receives a letter allegedly in Klamm's own
hand, stating that he is, 'as he knows', appointed
surveyor. The parenthesis seems to him a mockery

of his quest: it is not what he knows himself, but knowledge imparted by a superior knower, that he is in search of.

'The letter did not conceal that if it should come to a struggle K. had had the audacity to begin; this was referred to delicately, and only an unquiet conscience—an unquiet one, not a bad one—would notice it. It was the three words "as you know" referring to his acceptance into the service. K. had reported, and since then he knew, as the letter put it, that he was accepted' (p. 37). In short the letter, as K. reads it, tells him plainly that the knowledge he already has must be sufficient: if he looks for more it can only lead to a struggle which he, through his own dissatisfaction, has begun. Thus K.'s early attempts at establishing his identity come to grief. He is left with the possibly ambiguous designation, granted to him in the letter, of 'Vermesser'—both a surveyor, one who measures and plots out, sets limits and boundaries, and punningly ('sich vermessen') one who presumes, measures himself by false standards, makes too much of himself.[1]

K. is not disheartened by this rebuff. The search for external confirmation is of greater concern to him than it seems to be to the officials. His struggle is a purely personal one, whereas they act only as representatives of wills not their own: '... the officials, however well they might be organized, had only to defend, on behalf of distant, invisible masters, distant and invisible things, whereas K. was

[1] Cf. Erich Heller, *op. cit.* p. 169.

fighting for something vitally close, for himself' (p. 73).

K.'s personal interest in the progress of the struggle gives him an apparent slight advantage. Yet once again the castle appears to him in a dual aspect. Immediately following on this reflection comes another: ' . . . and not he alone was fighting for himself, but evidently other forces, which he did not know but in whom he could believe on account of the measures taken by the officials.' The castle appears then, not merely to be an enemy and a goal, but also to contain allies able to help K. For the present, he is only dimly conscious of this. He still demands success by virtue of his own efforts alone, 'auf eigene Faust'. The notion that there may be any real benevolence behind the castle's actions is only remotely present in his mind. The course of the plot reveals the gradual change in his attitude, whereby he comes first to submit himself to the castle, and finally to view it in a wholly different light.

IV

It has been maintained that *The Castle* is a novel in which there is no change, no metamorphosis. But this is not true, nor even a matter of the usual ambiguity found in Kafka's work. A simple narration of the development in K.'s relationships with the castle will make this plain.

K. arrives at the village in a confident mood, conscious of his own superiority and of his ability to succeed where others have failed. It is true that he has less presumptuousness than he had in the original (deleted) opening chapter, where he was shown on arrival straight into the 'Princes' Room', and gave himself such airs of authority that he almost at once broke into tears. The K. of the novel is much less neurotic than that, content with a sack on the floor for a bed, having a much more concealed form of morbid ambition, and only a small degree of persecution-mania. He is condescending to the landlord, patting him on the cheek to comfort him, fearful of the villagers, hiding beneath the blankets from their supposed wrath. He is gratified by respectful treatment from an official, sensitive to the slightest sign of mockery. Once he is assured of at least temporary lodging at the inn, he becomes suavely assured, disposing his affairs with the air of one quietly but efficiently picking out his path, and when he does break down it is not with weeping but in a kind of nervous weariness. For a man with a mission he is not far off normal.

K.'s confidence is of such a kind that it does not even trouble him to notice that the castle is not a castle in any ordinary sense of the word at all: 'It was neither an ancient fortress, nor a chateau, but a rambling construction consisting of a few double-storied buildings and a number of closely packed lower ones; if you had not known it was a castle you might have taken it for a little town' (p. 18).

Thus K.'s confidence relies on a traditional or pre-conceived notion of the castle's nature quite as much as does the confidence of the villagers, of which he is so distrustful. The castle is 'on the whole, just what K. expected' (p. 18). He has come with a conventional attitude, a reliance on the power of words to convey reality, that encloses him in his own subjectivity. The words 'if you had not known it was a castle' reveal K.'s naïve trust in accepting the designations provided by other people rather than the evidence of his own senses. The course of events undermines his confidence and his optimism until he relies solely on the attitude of complete scepticism and is finally reduced to indifference.

First, K. begins to be put off by the equally strong confidence and optimism of the villagers: the sight of it in other people is not encouraging, as the reader observes by looking, in his turn, at K. Then come the wearisome assurances of the castle's inaccessibility —the telephones are unreliable, the documents incalculable, the officials inscrutable. His own first attempt at reaching the castle on foot ends in a nervous physical exhaustion. It is not long before K. begins to look about for allies who will share his point of view, and he shortly imagines he has found one in the barmaid, Frieda. What attracts K. to Frieda is the belief that she is willing for his sake to abandon Klamm, whose mistress she has been, and to join him in offering defiance to the castle and all its ways. Whether this is in fact Frieda's intention is open to doubt: another interpretation is offered before the close of the novel. But that is how K. interprets her action, and his attempt at setting up house with her in the village, his acceptance of a job as school-caretaker (much against his will), are means to strengthen his confidence and opposition to authority. He has a tendency to use her love for him, and his for her, as a stalking-horse towards his goal. As a result, he seldom has any human contact with her or with anyone else.

K.'s confidence remains more or less unimpaired, despite the dissuasive efforts of the hostess at the Bridge Inn, the village elder, the schoolmaster, and K.'s personal failure to reach the castle, until the episode at the Herrenhof Inn, when K. spends half the night in a fruitless attempt to waylay Klamm and force him into a meeting face to face. Not until this time does K. ever feel biting shame and a sense of his own complete inferiority.

The change is heralded by the new impression made on K. by the castle, which he passes on his way to the Herrenhof. At first view he had called it 'a really miserable little town' (p. 18), scarcely superior to the place he had come from, his home. This had corresponded to his general assumption of easy acquaintanceship with the place. Now that he has experienced some of the difficulty in reaching it, his point of view is changing, and the castle accordingly appears to him in a different light:

'When K. looked at the castle it used to seem to him at times as though he were observing someone quietly sitting there gazing, not lost in thought and thereby shut off from everything, but free and untroubled, as though he were alone and observed by no one, but this did not disturb his quiet in the least. And sure enough—you couldn't tell whether as a cause or a consequence—an observer could not maintain his gaze, and let it slip aside. This impression was reinforced today by the early darkness; the longer he looked, the less he recognized, and the deeper everything was lost in the twilight' (p. 120).

The fact that K. is able to attribute this untroubled quality to the castle indicates some change in him. The reader only hears how the castle looks to one character or another: if its aspect to K. changes, that is significant. K. seems to be of the opinion now that to be lost in thought is to be 'shut off from everything'; since his approach has hitherto been cerebral and rational, he may be on the point of discovering the cause of the exclusiveness and isolation that has been his lot. But no more than on the point: the castle is now evidently, in K.'s own view, his superior. He is unable to withstand the untroubled gaze; there seems to be still some lack of sincerity in him.

K. goes on at once to the Herrenhof, where the scene just witnessed is repeated in terms of his relationship with Klamm. Klamm too sits upstairs in his room, silent and unanswering, waiting for K. to give up his concentrated purposefulness. He makes no more positive move than did the castle itself, but simply waits until K.'s gaze, as it were, slides away and he abandons his plan. K. realizes for the first time, with chagrin, his inferiority both to the castle and to Klamm, who now become almost identified in his mind, and for the first time also he begins to feel guilty towards both. It is the guilt of a man completely alone in the world, attempting to establish his values 'of his own will', and realizing that he is thereby, unlike the castle, 'shut off from everything'. The emotion is not without pleasure: there is some consolation in this Nietzschean situation. Sitting in Klamm's sleigh in the Herrenhof courtyard K. experiences the delights of this self-regarding pleasure; drinking Klamm's cognac he experiences a sweet and flattering sensation, as though some lover were praising him for qualities he did not know he possessed. Yet his narcissism is swiftly followed by feelings of guilt. An official appears at the door of the inn, K. starts up, lets fall his bottle, and remarks with 'disquiet' the slow dripping of the cognac on the running-board of the sleigh. He is ashamed, though the reason for his shame is never explicitly given, and may reside in a

concealed sexual suggestiveness which the scene has
—his narcissistic tendencies are both intellectual and
physical. At all events, he is conscious of self-reproach:
he looks at the official 'sullenly' ('düster'), 'but the look
was meant for himself' (p. 126).

The official insists that K. will fail to see Klamm
whether he goes or stays; Klamm's sledge is driven
back into a stable, and K. is left in almost total
obscurity, except for the one ray of light shining
through a crack in the gallery of the courtyard. The
ray of light indicates to him that he is not completely
abandoned even at this low point of his course: it is
linked with the description of the castle at the beginning of the chapter, for its function is to 'fix K.'s
wandering gaze a little' (p. 129). K. had not been
able to hold the gaze of the personified castle, and
now that he feels himself defeated by Klamm his
eyes lack almost all concentration. Only the still
remaining light is able to give any shape or form to
his intention now. In all other respects he is a weather-
cock at the mercy of every gust, rather than a magnet
steadily drawn towards its pole.

K. has now the kind of freedom for which he has
been fighting; at least he feels 'more free than he had
ever done before' (p. 129). At the same time, however,
his quite personal freedom from all compulsion of
tradition and environment cuts him off from all his
fellow-men, and inspires self-reproach. Together with
the sensation of freedom comes the equally strong
conviction 'that nothing could be so meaningless,
nothing so desperate as this freedom, this waiting,

46

this inviolability' (p. 129). K. is free in the way that Nietzsche was, or in the way that Kierkegaard described when he defined 'Angst' as 'the awareness of infinite possibility'. He realizes the conventionality of most human opinion and the fragility of any viewpoint that attempts to be rid of conventions. There is not much point in being free if it means the freedom to be shut up with yourself, and K. feels now that 'they had broken off all communication with him' (p. 129). He is proud of what he has achieved but at the same time recognizes the possibility of a different freedom which will join him in communion with other men. To quote Kierkegaard again (without asking whether Kafka had him consciously in mind): 'Freedom is constantly communicating . . .; unfreedom becomes more and more shut up and wants no communication.'[1]

K.'s realization that the castle is not his oyster, but exists in its own right, is revealed in his changed attitude towards Klamm. Formerly, when Klamm was compared to an eagle, and K. to a blindworm, K. had shrugged off the comparison. Now, like Job confronted with the Creator of Leviathan, he becomes aware of Klamm's absolute transcendence, and the impossibility of measuring him by any village standards:

'The hostess had once compared Klamm to an eagle, and that had seemed ridiculous to K., but not now; he thought of his distance, his impregnable dwelling-place, his dumbness, broken perhaps only

[1] Kierkegaard, *The Concept of Dread*, trans. Lowrie (London, 1944), p. 110.

by cries such as K. had never heard, of his downward piercing gaze that could never be verified, never be refuted, of those circlings in the air that could never be destroyed from out of K.'s depths, and in which he wheeled about up there in accordance with incomprehensible laws, visible only for moments at a time: all that was common to Klamm and the eagle' (p. 139).

This is a long way from K.'s earlier assumption that a meeting with Klamm might easily be arranged. It is impossible to say that no change is observable in him after this realization that Klamm's activities (like metaphysical statements) are not a matter for verification or refutation. K. is aware now that the extent of his knowledge is more limited than he had supposed, and that Klamm is immeasurably his superior.

There is no sudden reversal in K.'s attitude, however. There is after all nothing he can do, in the face of Klamm's immense transcendence, but to remain in his vortex. All that follows between this scene and the crucial interview with the official Bürgel, after which K.'s attitude undergoes a fundamental reorientation, shows K.'s sympathies being further and further alienated from the castle. He returns first to the school-house, where Frieda is waiting for him, and comforts himself with the reflection that here at least he has established a home where he can do some useful work—a ridiculously optimistic view of his purely human situation, soon to be undermined by the riotous confusion of the following morning. He is not even able to comfort himself with the possession of a wife for long, for Frieda, whose sympathies remain attached to the castle, unaccountably turns away from him to defend the childish antics of K.'s irresponsible assistants. Believing that she prefers their company to his own, K. abandons her and takes refuge in the house of the Barnabas family. Frieda is not the like-minded helpmate he had hoped for, who would enable him to establish a communion of love without need of the castle's help. She drives him yet further into his isolation.

The story of the Barnabas family, as related by Olga, presents the castle in an increasingly repulsive light. It is from Olga, the sister of K.'s personal messenger Barnabas, that K. hears the account of the senselessly cruel punishment that followed on the refusal of the other sister, Amalia, to conform with the official Sortini's demands. K.'s alienation, and the reader's, can only be strengthened on hearing of Olga's and Barnabas's transparently honest attempts to rehabilitate the family in the eyes of village and castle. The officials and the castle organization begin now to look implacable.

In the main, the attitude represented by Barnabas is one of complete and infinite scepticism. (The attitude of Olga, which is different, must be left aside for the moment.) There is even something comic about the profound distrust with which Barnabas considers every event connected with the castle, a distrust which is matched only by that of K. himself. Barnabas alone of all the villagers has regular access to the castle, yet he alone is doubtful about the value of this privilege:

'Is it castle work at all that Barnabas is doing?' asks Olga. 'It's true, he goes into the offices, but are the offices the actual castle? And even if there are offices belonging to the castle, are they the offices that Barnabas is allowed to enter? He goes into offices, but they are only a part of the whole, then come barriers and behind them there are other offices. . . . And then the doubt continues, you can't help yourself. Barnabas speaks to officials, Barnabas receives messages. But what sort of officials, what sort of messages are they? At present he is, he says, assigned to Klamm, and receives instructions direct from him. . . . Think of it, being directly assigned to Klamm, speaking with him mouth to mouth. But is it so? Well yes, it is, but why does Barnabas doubt that the official, who is called Klamm there, really is Klamm?' (p. 204).

This is the kind of doubt that can never be refuted, any more than certainties about Klamm can be refuted. Without allegorizing in the slightest, it can be said that Barnabas is concerned here with purely meta-physical questions of reality, of a kind which, as positivist philosophers demonstrate, is simply not open to empirical proof or disproof. Barnabas is strictly logical about all this: as K. observes to Olga when she has finished her account, 'How astonishingly clearly you think'—the remark might apply to all the family, and to K. himself into the bargain. However much evidence you offered to Barnabas that the Klamm he met was really Klamm, the offices he entered were the real offices, he would always be able to claim that the evidence was incomplete. He can give

you no definition of what Klamm *is* really like, but
he will always be right in asserting that Klamm is not
necessarily as he sees him. If you are not sympathizing
with him at the moment, you find his attitude comical.
Certainty, it has been observed, is having your eyes
closed to doubt, and even Barnabas can be certain at
times: he has no hesitation in recognizing the official
Erlanger when it comes to the point, nor in recognizing the acquaintances of his normal everyday life.
His doubts are reserved for the castle and Klamm.
It almost looks as though he fears certainty, just as
K. hears in the sound of the castle bells a *threat* of
'fulfilment of that for which he was uncertainly
longing' (p. 27). Evidently K., if he were to enter the
castle in his present frame of mind, would be assailed
by doubts just as strong and just as far-reaching as
those of Barnabas. Both he and Barnabas are dissatisfied because what they see is 'only part of the whole'.
Their modesty is a useful corrective to bigotry and
an essential realization of their condition.

The episode of the Barnabas family, seen in this
aspect, is not, then, a demonstration of the folly of
reasoning. That is a matter of your mood. Once
reasoning begins, as Olga observes, 'the doubts continue, you can't help yourself'. Barnabas is a likeable
character, and the reader's sympathies, like K.'s, are
driven more and more during Olga's narration on to
her side, at the sight of her courage, her continuing
hope in the face of all odds, her charitableness and
her self-sacrifice. She is infinitely anxious to believe
the castle in the right, and this very anxiety strengthens

the impression that the castle is in the wrong. Offered the choice between the villagers' cheerful and un-reasoning claim to absolute knowledge, and Olga's desperate, rational claim to absolute ignorance, K. can only side with her. On the other hand, the fuller realization of his condition does not produce in K. the 'good-naturedness' which he notices as one of the chief characteristics of the family. He is so alienated from the castle now that he takes a willow-rod and goes out to whip the assistants back where they came from. He no longer feels any need for them: his feeling of guilt and inferiority towards the castle has transformed itself into hatred.

The events leading up to this point, seen mainly from the attitude of a sceptic, present an intensification of K.'s defiance towards the castle and a weakening of his determination to enter it, as well as of his awareness of the castle's transcendence. By now he has apparent-ly given up all intention of meeting Klamm face to face, partly because he realizes it is impossible, partly because he revolts against the whole castle system. It is conceivable, of course, and this point will have to be examined later, that it was part of Klamm's purpose to bring K. to this situation. But as far as K. is con-cerned at the moment, he is confronted by a petty bureaucracy in the control of self-satisfied and tyran-nical officials whose actions are either laughable or monstrous.

The interview with Bürgel, however, still lies ahead. The events following Olga's narrative serve to intro-duce it, and at the same time indicate a subtle change in K. He thinks, in fact, that he is about to dismiss his assistants; in reality they are already handing in their resignations, and the passage in which this is revealed has some significance. Leaving the Barnabas home, K. meets the assistant Jeremiah who has come in search of him, and learns that Arthur, the other assistant, has gone back to the castle to lodge a complaint on behalf of them both:

'"And you?" K. asked. "I was able to stay," said Jeremiah, "Arthur is complaining for me too." "What are you complaining about then?" asked K. "About you not understanding a joke", said Jeremiah. "What have we done? Joked a bit, laughed a bit, teased your fiancée a bit. And all in accordance with instructions. When Galatian sent us to you—" "Galatian?" asked K. "Yes, Galatian", said Jeremiah. "He was deputizing for Klamm then. When he sent us to you, he said . . . 'The main thing is to cheer him up a little. From what I have been told he takes everything very hard. He has come into the village now, and straight away he takes that for a very great event, whereas in reality it is nothing at all. Make him see that.'" "Well," said K., "was Galatian right, and have you done what he told you?" "I don't know", said Jeremiah' (p. 269).

As a matter of fact, K. has been considerably humbled since he first arrived at the village. But looking at the meaningless antics of the assistants you wonder how they imagined they might be bringing this about; you incline to agree with K. and to share his astonishment at Frieda's defence of them. But if you suppose for a moment that their antics are

53

not meaningless, that the assistants have carried out their instructions precisely and have every reason to complain, sense emerges. There is for instance the scene at the Bridge Inn after K. has had his first glimpse of Klamm through a hole in the door, and fancies that by winning Frieda's allegiance he has gained some kind of victory. In K.'s room the assistants curl themselves up in a corner, affecting the greatest respect for K.'s status, and playing childish games. They pretend to use their hands as telescopes, or comb their beards and ask Frieda to decide which of them has the longer and fuller (p. 59). K. watches all this with grave indifference. If he had more sense of humour he might suppose that the assistants were mimicking his own Paul Prying, squinting through Klamm's keyhole, and his own childish self-importance—'who has the biggest one?' They act in a similar way after K. has spent the night in his fruitless effort to waylay Klamm, waiting for hours in the snow to draw the official's attention to himself. On the following night, K. drives the assistants out into the snow of the school playground, and next morning one of the pair is still there, waving his arms, rolling his eyeballs, yearning like mad for K. to come out to him, even hitching himself by his coat on to the railing-spikes to affirm his inflexible purpose. The assistants enact one long parody of K.'s persistence, they are a standing invitation to take someone else's view for a change. It is natural enough for K. to overlook their exaggerated reflection of his secret egoism. When he has just been reclining in bed, weakly allowing them to rush up and downstairs fetching water and soap, comb and mirror, languidly indicating that he would like a little glass of rum, he has no idea why they should nudge each other into showing respect, or end up by saluting him. He does not observe that after he has stolen Klamm's mistress the assistants steal his. And because the story is told from K.'s point of view none of this ever becomes explicit. The nearest approach to explicitness is when K. reflects, in the Herrenhof courtyard: 'if only he had sent his assistants here; even they would have managed to act as he had done' (p. 126). For the rest, the onus of reflection remains with the reader. It is the reader who observes that the assistants act so as to heighten K.'s self-awareness at every turn. They are present even (or rather, above all) at K.'s most intimate moments, goading him all the time into consciousness of what he is doing. But evidently, they are not able to tell K. their function in so many words: he must realize for himself the extent and absurdity of this apparent *hubris*. Only then will he realize that his entry into the village was not of the slightest importance.

Have the assistants succeeded? Jeremiah says he does not know. The most one can say is that K. is at least aware now of his insignificance in comparison with the castle, and that on the whole he has lost his desire to enter it or gain a victory over it. The fact that the assistants are now leaving him may, however, be interpreted in two ways. It could indicate equally well that K. is so humbled as to have no more need

of the assistants, or that his inability to see the point
of their satire has made of him a hopeless case. There
is no point in mocking either a madman or a saint.
(Lear's Fool may be felt to abandon his master in
kindred circumstances: his parody of kingship is no
longer fitting.) K. is either so self-disregarding that
he can dispense with the assistants, or so self-centred
that their efforts are in vain. At the same time, the
possibility that the castle has a fundamentally benevolent attitude towards K. begins to emerge for the
first time.

V

There can be no question that K., in his present mood of detachment from the castle, hatred for the assistants, and defiant unconcern about the end of his quest, is different from the dogged seeker after confirmation with whom the novel began. But the change does not amount to a transformation, there is nothing much remarkable about it. The metamorphosis itself does not in fact come about until after the climax, the interview with the official Bürgel.

It is immediately after the conversation with Jeremiah that K. receives, through Barnabas, the invitation which leads to this interview. The language in which the invitation is couched is in itself worth attention. It is not a direct command but much more of a friendly request: 'You know the land-surveyor, don't you?' [an official has inquired of Barnabas.] 'That's lucky, I'm just going to drive in to the Herrenhof. Tell the land-surveyor to come and see me there. I live in room number fifteen. But he would need to come right away. I only have a few interviews there and shall be driving back at five in the morning. Tell him it matters a lot to me to speak with him' (p. 275).

This has none of the abruptness K. has come to expect of the castle, nothing of the humiliating order to Amalia. It even sounds as though the official is more concerned to meet K. than K. is to meet him.

Indeed the official's name itself might suggest this. Erlanger (who issues the request, though it is not he that meets K.) has a name that might be found in any German telephone directory. At the same time, however, as Erich Heller has observed, it might be derived from the verb 'erlangen', and thus imply 'the one who attains'. Hitherto, all effort at 'attaining' has been on K.'s side. The new name, together with the message, might be taken to mean that this official, at least, needs K. as much as K. needs the castle, that a mutual process of completion is involved. It may appear that K.'s success is desired as much by the castle, for its own sake, as it is by K. for his own, and that the 'attainment' is not an exclusive goal of either the one or the other. This is a lot to base on a fairly friendly message and an esoteric pun which might not even have been intended. It will look more justifiable when the ensuing events are seen in more detail.

Curiously enough K., despite his defiance, is off like a shot to the Herrenhof as soon as the invitation arrives. It is not of course Erlanger that he meets, but Bürgel, into whose room he stumbles by accident. Yet Bürgel does present to K. just that dependence on K.'s persistence that is suggested by the name of Erlanger. Bürgel has a strangely dual attitude towards K. He both fears and welcomes his unexpected arrival, regarding it as an invitation to do battle just as K. formerly regarded the challenge of the castle. He speaks as though, from the moment K. enters his room, it becomes possible for him, Bürgel, to liberate himself from his position, while at the same time he is full of fear at the prospect:

'Of course, once the applicant is in the room it's pretty bad. It's a weight on your heart. "How long can you put up a resistance?" you ask yourself. But there won't be any resistance, you know that. Just try and imagine the situation as it really is. The applicant you have never seen, always expected, expected with a veritable thirst, and whom you have always regarded quite rationally as being unattainable, is there, sitting in front of you' (p. 309).

K., by this account, has represented just such an inaccessible goal to the officials (Bürgel relates his own account as being typical of them all) as they have seemed to him. Each is, epigrammatically, the other's castle; there is thirst on both sides. Eventually, moreover, while K. is undoubtedly transformed, it is Bürgel who shows the clearest external signs of rejuvenation as a result of this meeting. It seems that without K.'s struggle, or the struggle of others like him, the officials could never reach their own ultimate goal.

That is not K.'s view of the matter: he is not in a position to compare his own attitude with that of the officials. As far as K. is concerned, he expects nothing at all from the castle now, though he hurries to the interview for all that. He is no longer concerned with saving himself, any more than with liberating the officials. His reception at the Herrenhof, where the usual castle nonsense is in full swing, does nothing to inspire his confidence. The wretched villagers, also

called out in the middle of the night for interviews
with the same official, are waiting in the snow outside,
inventing every possible reason why they should be
so inconvenienced. K. is received by Momus, the
self-satisfied clerk whose namesake in classical myth-
ology was the mocker of the gods, and who now
mocks at K.'s eagerness for an interview which before
he had vehemently rejected. Even Frieda, whom K.
meets inside, refuses to marry him, presents him with
the left-overs of someone else's meal, and goes off
to care for Jeremiah in her room. K. is left 'aimlessly
gazing about' having no longer any purpose at all,
rejecting even the temptation to win back Frieda's
sympathy.

It is in these circumstances and in this frame of
mind that K. stumbles into Bürgel's room, where the
suggestion of a possible escape from his dilemma is
placed in his mind, only to pass by disregarded. The
name this time, to quote Erich Heller again, suggests
a diminutive of 'Bürge', guarantor,—'the little official
who offers the solution, without K. even noticing the
chance'.[1] Bürgel does in fact offer a solution, or at
least he seems to guarantee that there *is* a solution. The
most important question for the whole novel, however, is to ask what this solution amounts to, and what
is to be made of K.'s failure to respond to it. On this
depends the answer to the claim that nothing effective
comes of the interview.

As usual, the first impressions are discouraging.
Bürgel's first reaction to K.'s entry is to hide under

[1] Erich Heller, *op. cit.* p. 170.

the bedclothes, his second, to begin a long patter of words ostensibly addressed to K., which Bürgel hopes will send him back to his broken sleep. His appearance, childish and self-satisfied, is not reassuring either. The effect of his talk, however—is it intentional?—is to induce sleep not in himself but K., who is simply too weary to pay attention.

The mention of this sleep is an opportunity to quote a commentary on this scene, by Idris Parry, which is so close to the mark as to almost persuade. Mr Parry's view is that in falling asleep K. achieves his triumph:

'The superb artistry of this incident becomes apparent if we realize that the story is still being told from K.'s point of view, though he is unconscious. It is because he is unconscious, given over to nature, that his triumph is possible. He has indeed stumbled into this opportunity in all helplessness. He is not aware of success, but unawareness is the pre-requisite of revelation. This is the profoundest irony of all, the ironical situation of man, successful only when he stops trying to succeed. When K. awakens he is still fallibly human, but Kafka has brilliantly symbolized the way to salvation without violating the truth that it can never be apparent to K.'s imperfect human consciousness.'[1]

I find a great deal to sympathize with in these lines, which in fact gave an initial impulse to the present study. It is only on the question of K.'s unconsciousness that I have any need to dissent. Mr Parry's words suggest that K.'s triumph is in the brief moments of

[1] Idris Parry, in a review in *The London Magazine*, May 1954, p. 80.

sleep which occur during the interview, that there is no success for him in his normal waking life but only in the world of dreams. I do not think, and did not think when I first read these lines, that that is a satisfying solution, nor do I think it is a plausible interpretation of the events. K. is 'unaware', yes, but he is not 'unconscious' when the real climax comes.

K. does in fact dream during the interview, and the events of the dream are like a reflection on the fatuity of most dreams. K., still half-conscious, imagines that a great crowd is toasting his victory over a naked secretary, who confronts him like the statue of a Greek god:

'It was very funny, and K. smiled gently at it in his sleep, to see the secretary being startled out of his proud posture by K.'s attacks, having to use his uplifted arm or his clenched fist to cover up, and still being too slow. The fight did not last long; step by step, and they were big steps at that, K. advanced. Was it a fight at all? There was no serious obstacle, only an occasional squeak from the secretary. This Greek god was squealing like a girl being tickled. And at last he was gone, K. was alone in the great room; in fighting trim he turned about and sought his opponent. But there was no one there, the people had gone too, only the champagne glass lay broken on the floor. K. stamped it to bits. But the fragments cut him; with a start he awoke after all, and felt as sick as a little child that has been wakened' (p. 304).

K. in the role of he-man is too good to be true. In his waking moments he would never accept such a blatant piece of wish-fulfilment as the answer to his quest. If the scene were meant seriously as a symbol of the 'way to salvation' (though this cannot have been in Mr Parry's mind when he wrote of K.'s unconscious triumph) it would be blasphemous, like the very similar scene in Greene's *Heart of the Matter*.[1] The freedom which K. is said to feel as this dream begins is as pointless as his apparent victory over Klamm at the Herrenhof, or as the adventure of his schoolboy days when he climbed a wall to triumph over the graveyard—'here and now nobody was greater than he'—and was scared off by his teacher (p. 42). But the fight with the secretary does more than illustrate the absurdity of K.'s dream, it also reveals K.'s subconscious attitude to all talk of struggling with the castle and achieving victory over it. He smiles at the notion even in his sleep, and, unlike the memory of his schooldays, the dream has a decidedly comic twist. This is significant for later developments.

It is in the second half of the Bürgel interview, after K.'s reawakening, that events of more considerable importance take place. Bürgel goes on to explain that night-time interviews are in themselves more profitable than others, and not only this: the only way in which a supplicant can hope to achieve success is by chancing to meet an official late at night, an official who is not competent to deal with his case, and with whom no interview has been arranged—all circumstances which fit K.'s case exactly. Evidently K. has only to put his question and all will be over, but he

[1] Cf. Graham Greene, *The Heart of the Matter* (London, 1948), p. 256.

hangs back, incapable from sheer weariness. Bürgel rambles on, explaining the legal aspects of the case, claiming like the village elder that no exceptions are ever made, but hinting that 'the complete improbability may suddenly take shape'. He comments on the fears an official may have in circumstances like these, and on the ardent desire that the supplicant may at last be attained. The real battle seems about to be joined, not the sham one where K. dreamed his way to victory, and the opportunity of victory hangs over K. like a ripe fruit.

Bürgel supplies further evidence that K.'s quest involves a mutual process in himself and in the castle. If, he says, an official should take it upon himself to grant a request under these totally exceptional conditions—a measure which would destroy the whole organization of the castle—it would imply a claim on his part to 'a promotion in rank passing all conception'. Evidently, if Bürgel were to meet with such an occasion, as he does now, he would be freeing himself, raising his status to the nth degree. On the other hand, he goes on to explain that the interviewed party himself would then also be in a like position. Having arrived 'exhausted, disappointed, unfeeling and indifferent', he must now be told that in all his helplessness 'he can control everything' (p. 311). This places K.'s potential status, if the words are taken in all their literal senses, quite as high as that of Bürgel. If 'the most improbable thing' were to come about, both might become, in Hamlet's phrase, 'kings of infinite space'. It is K.'s quest that has made possible this intensification of the diametrically opposed forces to a point where their power can become equal. The realization of the mystic's dream could not be proffered more plainly. But of course K. misses his chance by falling asleep at the very moment when Bürgel is waiting for him to put his question.

There is no victory; K.'s weariness continues. Does this mean, though, that he has failed? The immediate assumption is that, like Parsifal before the Holy Grail, he erred in not seizing his advantage. But suppose K. had in fact asked the question as Bürgel invited him to do. Would this not have been to succumb to the greatest and subtlest temptation of all? To act now, in the belief that one's action would result in the highest possible personal aggrandizement, would be a relapse into K.'s earliest state of self-centred striving. The temptation is all the stronger because he is so hopeless now, and has undergone so much spiritual conflict to arrive in his present condition. Surely after all this, he might have argued, he was entitled to such a reward. Bürgel makes it so easy for him, appearing not to realize the aptness to K.'s case of what he is saying, encouraging K. to believe that the situation is entirely in K.'s hands and that the castle is at his mercy. It is so convincing that the reader himself is inclined to be sorry for K.'s incapacity. K., however, without any suggestion of merit, neither accepts nor consciously rejects—he is past caring. Not that he has stopped listening, or fails to see what Bürgel is driving at: '... he did indeed notice that what Bürgel was talking about probably concerned him very much, but he now had a great dislike of things that concerned him . . .' (p. 301). This lack of self-concern is obviously, though not explicitly, the reason why K. does not seize power when it is offered to him.

It does not matter, then, whether what Bürgel tells K. is literally true. Kafka had no need of the fragment, now published with the deletions, in which people assert that Bürgel is a mere nobody with no real knowledge of castle secrets. (This piece, related in a tone of spiteful gossip, must have been rejected also because it would have been the one passage in the whole book of which K. could have had no knowledge: it is incongruous because it is not a conversation heard by K.) What does matter is that in this moment of utter helplessness and hopelessness K. does not clutch at the straw, thinking it might give him absolute power and bring the whole castle system into collapse. He does not exploit his desperate position.

This is the point, as K.'s head 'hangs free' in sleep, when the summons to meet Erlanger actually comes. It has not come in the way K. expected, but it does come, and he does see Erlanger after all. At the precise moment when Bürgel is waiting expectantly for K.'s question, and K. is failing to put it, there is a loud knocking on the partition wall and Erlanger's voice is heard. 'Is the land-surveyor there?' he calls, though he can scarcely have guessed this since K. has hardly spoken a word and has been silent for some time past. 'Then tell him it's high time he came over here'. ('Dann soll er endlich herüberkommen.') Is this an expression of angry impatience, as Bürgel suggests, without consideration for K., or is it a recognition that the time has arrived for K. to 'come over'? K. is not concerned with this kind of doubt now; he leaves Bürgel's room because it seems quite useless to stay there any longer, but not, even now, because he thinks he has gained anything by his inactivity. Meeting Erlanger in the corridor outside he does receive the first definite order he has ever had, to carry out on Klamm's behalf, but even this seems to him like a mockery.

It does seem, then, that the interview has ended in total failure. K. has neither gained any victory nor profited by his lack of desire for personal aggrandizement. But this is to reckon without the events which follow on the Bürgel interview and the brief meeting with Erlanger. It soon becomes clear that K., for all his continuing weariness has become quite a different man. His attitude towards the castle has changed entirely. Standing in the corridor outside Erlanger's room he begins to feel an absurdly elated admiration for the castle officials working behind their partitions. He compares his own weariness with theirs, and concludes: ' . . . in its way it was a quite different weariness from his own. Here no doubt it was weariness in the midst of cheerful work; something that outwardly looked like weariness, and was actually indestructible repose, indestructible peace. If you are a little tired at noon, that is all in the natural course of a happy day's work. These gentlemen have continual noon, K. said to himself' (p. 315).

This is almost like the kind of language which K. used to hear from the villagers, when they used to praise the castle. But it is also significantly different. K. is not uttering a contradiction; he is not saying that the castle is both completely efficient and liable to error, or that it is at one and the same time hostile and friendly. He is, rather, uttering a paradox in the better sense of the word—a seemingly absurd though perhaps well-founded statement. Moreover he is not trying to prove that the officials always act with propriety or omniscience, he is merely impressed with their peace. Contrast with this K.'s reception after the scene in the Herrenhof courtyard. Then, the landlord had greeted him dumbly, the landlady had been 'an oppressive sight for K.', he was greeted with cold indifference on all sides. Now, with no new evidence to alter his point of view, and with nothing but the voices of the invisible officials to go by, K. appreciates everything freshly:

'This babble of voices in the rooms had something extremely joyful about it. At one moment it would sound like the rejoicing of children getting ready for an outing, at another, like the first stirrings in a hen-house, like the joy of being in complete harmony with the awakening day—somewhere one of the gentle-men even imitated the crowing of a cock' (p. 315). There is an odd blend here of comedy and splendour: a phrase like 'the joy of being in complete harmony with the awakening day' comes strangely in this context, though it does not conflict with it. The castle has always tended to reflect K.'s moods and expec-

68

tations; it begins to look as though his expectation has changed.

K.'s attitude continues to show this warm appoval towards the events that follow. As a servant comes down the corridor handing out documents for the day's work, K. looks on 'not only with curiosity, but also with sympathy'. His weariness, moreover, has either disappeared or is no longer of much account to him, since he feels 'almost well amid the coming and going'. K. never enjoyed such well-being or sympathy with the castle before. To call it euphoria is to display a scientific detachment from his mood.

Despite his approval, K. is not entirely on the side of the officials. The episode which he witnesses, where the servant hands out the documents to various occupants along the corridor, presents his equally great sympathy with those who oppose the bureau-cracy and insist on having their own way. A complete parallel to his own actions is now presented before K.'s eyes. There is some difficulty about the distri-bution: some of the documents have gone to the wrong rooms and the officials refuse to give them back. K. observes and admires the way the servant goes to work. He fights against these invisible, un-attainable officials behind their closed doors, will not accept their silence or their refusal, grows weary, gives up the direct approach and tries cunning, pretends not to be interested and then returns with twice the energy, and at last forces the official con-cerned to 'deal with him face to face' (p. 320). These have been precisely K.'s methods in dealing with the

officials, and the conclusion, that they lead at least
to a 'semi-satisfactory result', might well be applied
by him to his own case. So too might K.'s view that
the servant has 'probably acted in just the right way'.
But the notable point here is that K. is no longer
concerned with an introspective or retrospective review of his past and present actions. His attention is
turned entirely outwards and away from himself. If
he cared to look back at the past he might say, 'If
I had not been so insistent in my demands I should not
have acquired this present well-being and sympathy,
any more than this servant, had he been less tenacious,
would have had the pleasure of distributing his
documents.' He could, in short, justify himself. But
'qui s'excuse s'accuse'. The insistence which K. finds
justifiable is not his own but another person's; he is
able to judge these actions far more favourably than
he ever did his own. Similarly, it is to the officials
that K. ascribes the feelings of joy, complete harmony,
and indestructible peace. The fact that he himself is
full of approval and sympathy, or that he is in harmony both with the officials and with the insistent servant does not occur to him as significant. A remark of
Yeats's in his old age is apposite here: 'It seems to me
that I have found what I wanted. When I try to put
it all into a phrase I say "Man can embody truth but
he cannot know it." I must embody it in the completion of my life. The abstract is not life and everywhere drags out its contradictions. You can refute
Hegel but not the Saint or the Song of Sixpence.'[1]

[1] R. Ellmann, *Yeats: The Man and the Masks* (London, 1949), p. 289.

The difference between K. and Yeats, on this point, is that K. is not even trying to embody truth; he does not ask whether he has found what he wanted and is quite unaware of any problem, so the possibility of refutation does not arise. 'Truth is indivisible, and so cannot recognize itself; anyone who would recognize it must be a lie.' [1]

Still untroubled by personal reflections, K. now watches the final action of the servant as the man finds himself left with one document for which there is no recipient. It occurs to K. that this might very well be the document referring to his own case. Noticeably, he does not *think* this—he seems not to be doing much thinking now—it 'passes through K.'s head'. Feeling rather ridiculous he tries to draw nearer and find out, but without success, for almost at once the servant tears up the document and puts the pieces in his pocket. On the face of it, it might well look as though K.'s case were concluded. He has been reduced during the novel to complete hopelessness, a recognition of the absolute transcendence of the castle's ways; he has withstood the temptation to accept Bürgel's offer and has perhaps been rewarded by his fresh attitude towards everyone about him. The servant, whose actions have paralleled his own hitherto, now ends with an action that is, in Bürgel's language, 'completely irregular'. It seems as though there is no need to continue correspondence about K., no official is required to occupy himself with the case any longer. —But is this 'really' what has happened? Is the small-

[1] Kafka, *Tagebücher, ed. cit.* p. 210 (Wer Sie anerkennen will, muß Lüge sein').

ness of the document—a scrap of paper is all it is—an indication that K. had already progressed so far that little more needed to be said about him and his dossier was reduced to this dimension? Or does the size merely indicate the triviality of the whole matter? Does the destruction mean that K. is above reproach or beyond contempt? Is it even K.'s document at all? Earlier, K. would have been desperately concerned to get at the truth of this, and would have raised a good many more doubts than I have been able to find. Now, it is a mark of his attitude that it does not trouble him in the slightest. The notion passes through his head and never recurs; the small effort that he does make to find out seems to him 'arbitrary and ridiculous'. To make any further effort would be to begin all over again the search for absolute confirmation which he has already given up as hopeless. He gets certainty when he has given up wanting it, or to put it another way he ceases to doubt as soon as he ceases to want a quasi-divine rightness or to place any absolute dependence on his own powers. Thus neither K. nor anybody else is entitled to say that by the tearing up of the document his case is concluded, let alone concluded favourably. The important point is not whether K.'s case is concluded but that he is no longer concerned to know. This writes *finis* to K.'s case more cogently than any speculation about the nature of unknowables. K.'s transformation stares the reader in the face, it is a perceivable spiritual reality, not, like the nature of the document, a matter for reasonable doubt.

The reader is now the one who is in a difficult position. If he continues to inquire whether these events have any 'real' significance he adopts K.'s earlier attitude. Only by himself ceasing to be concerned can he accept the transformed K.'s attitude as real enough. And there is something of Barnabas's infinite scepticism in most readers of Kafka: we would like to know beyond the faintest shadow of a doubt. Yet this kind of knowledge is just what is presented in the picture of K. now. In his present mood K. has many features of what we normally call, within the ordinary use of language, a good man, who has no need to quest any further. To doubt this is to take up the position characterized aptly by John Wisdom:

'One who says "No man is good—not even St Francis" may still be using words so that it is not impossible that a man should be good. But he may not be. For he may be so using the words "good" and "human" that a creature with evil desires is not good even if he overcomes them while one without such desires isn't human. Then his paradox couldn't be false.'[1] As Wisdom observes, one who has such an attitude towards human goodness is misleading, 'for he is not contrasting men with anything that could be in earth or heaven'.

'But this doesn't make what he says meaningless. For in his caricature of our idea of goodness he has brought out the conflicting elements in that idea by accentuating them until the hidden conflict becomes a contradiction and sweet perfection wears a foolish

[1] *Other Minds* (Oxford, 1952), pp. 257-8.

73

smile.'[1] This caricature of K. may still be made. But to do so requires an almost hostile frame of mind, and a determination that he shall wear a foolish smile. It is an attitude which is illustrated in the reactions to K. of some of the characters later in the chapter.

As the servant moves away with the torn-up document in his pocket, one of the officials, whose impatience has got out of hand, begins to ring an electric bell. Other officials chime in, and a peal of bells rings out, 'not of necessity now, but for sport and in an overflow of joy' (p. 323–'jetzt nicht mehr aus Not' where 'Not' means both 'necessity, need, compulsion', and 'exigency, distress'). The landlord and his wife come running down the corridor to lead K. away, the hubbub increases as the officials stream out of the rooms behind K.'s back, and 'through all this resounded the bells, pressed time and again, as though to celebrate a victory'. K. does not object when the landlord leads him away, in fact he approves of this as much as of everything else–'Because it mattered a great deal to him to understand wherein his guilt lay, he was very much in agreement when the landlord took him by the arm and went off with him away from all this noise'–This is the situation, then, as K. sees it: the officials are no longer under compulsion but free to rejoice and to celebrate a victory. He does not ask whether they are rejoicing over the one sinner who has returned home or at the defeat of his own aspirations, but is still concerned to know the nature of his guilt. K. shortly hears what a hostile or critical

[1] *Other Minds* (Oxford, 1952), pp. 257-8.

mind can make of these same events. The landlord
and his wife are outraged at K.'s audacity, standing
there in the corridor in flesh and blood while the
officials were trying to get on with their work. He
has shown the highest degree of irreverence by staying
on with his hands in his pockets, 'in all his natural
truth' (p. 326–'in aller Naturwahrheit'.). Only K.'s
presence in the corridor caused the dislocation of the
distributing system and the refusal of the officials to
open their doors to the servant; the ringing of the
bells was a desperate summons to the landlord to
take K. away. K. offers no defence to this, except to
say that he was utterly weary. It has become apparent
by now that all these conflicting interpretations are
a matter of personal attitude, and this is emphasized
now in K.'s response to his accusers.

'"But what had he done?", K. kept on asking, but
received no answer for a long while, because guilt
was too much a matter of course for both of them
['weil die Schuld den beiden allzu selbstverständlich
war'], so that they did not even remotely think of
his good faith ['und sie daher an seinen guten
Glauben nicht im entferntesten dachten']. (p. 323).
The premiss of the landlord is that 'natural truth'
must be offensive to the officials, that they cannot
bear the sight of flesh and blood in their corridors,
and that all applicants must *ipso facto* be guilty. Like
many of the characters in *The Trial*, he holds firmly by
'the law', and is shocked by K.'s seeming presumptuousness in 'setting himself above the law'. Similarly
the landlord's wife, a little later, accuses K. of not

speaking the truth: '"What are you then really?" "A land-surveyor." "What's that then?" K. explained; the explanation made her yawn. "You aren't speaking the truth. Why don't you speak the truth?" "You don't speak the truth either."' (p. 360)

Both landlord and wife represent an attitude of mind that is convinced of its own propriety and correctness. K.'s reply is that of a man resigned to his own limited standpoint. He does not argue the case as he used to do. He is at long last full of certainty—'completely convinced, almost to the point of being indifferent about it, that he would remain' (p. 329). (And, incidentally, this certainty comes long before the arrival of the official permit to stay in the village, which according to Max Brod was to have been described in the concluding, unwritten pages.) As far as the interviews are concerned, he confesses that he was 'almost in a kind of intoxication'. But, remarkably enough, he adds that 'everything went off very well, as far as he knows' (p. 328). This is K.'s 'good faith', and it is all there is to set against the malice of the landlord. K. has given up the attempt at penetrating beneath the surface of realities and events, just as he has given up the attempt at reaching the castle. There is only the surface to go by, and all interpretation reflects, as the castle itself reflects, the good faith or bad faith of the interpreter.

K. has not suddenly become immune to temptation. He permits himself some exaggeration when he talks to the landlord of his interviews, and is duly rewarded by a look of respect in the landlord's eyes (p. 329).

But this is one of the neatest and most generous touches by the author in the whole book. It provides that inevitable trace of pride in K., that slightest degree of awareness of what has happened, without which he would scarcely be human or credible. Again, when he goes out into the taproom and meets the new barmaid Pepi, he is not above making a pass at her. He remains a human being, not a sexless, passionless ascetic.

Nor is K.'s indifference, or near-indifference, a form of apathy: he has not given up his critical habits. In the final chapter, which is almost entirely taken up by a discussion between K. and Pepi, it becomes evident that he is not in a benignly condoning frame of mind. Pepi's main purpose is to decry her predecessor, Frieda, and present herself as a much more suitable object for Klamm's affections. K. hears her out, only to observe in the way he has always been accustomed to do the contradictions in her statement, the evasions and protestations, the half-admissions and temporizing equivocations: 'These are nothing but dreams from your dark, narrow maids' room downstairs, which are all very well down there, but look odd up here in the freedom of the taproom ['im freien Ausschank']. With thoughts like that you couldn't hold your position up here, that goes without saying' (p. 351).

The taproom, rather than the castle, has now become the place of freedom, and it is also a place where an attitude such as K. has seems to be at home. Pepi, he believes, is 'deceived because she wants to be deceived'. For his own part, he prefers Frieda's word to Pepi's:

'It is true—just as we are sitting here next to one another and I take your hand between mine, so Klamm and Frieda must have sat next to one another as though it were the most natural thing in the world, and he came down of his own free will, in fact he hurried down, there was nobody lurking in the corridor for him and neglecting their work, Klamm had to take the trouble of coming down himself, and the faults in Frieda's clothing, that would have horrified you, didn't trouble him in the least. And you won't believe her! You don't know how you show yourself up, how by that very fact you reveal your lack of experience' (p. 354).

There is no longer any jealousy or animosity towards Klamm, such as K. displayed earlier. Nor is there any final proof that K.'s present attitude corresponds with the facts. His conviction is expressed in these terms: 'I don't know whether it is so, but that it is rather so than the way you [Pepi] put it, I know for certain' (p. 355). He has arrived at an attitude which can be expressed, with reservations, in the religious terms of Kierkegaard: 'Within the individual man there is a potentiality . . . which is awakened in inwardness to become a God-relationship, and then it becomes possible to see God everywhere.' [1]

It is in K.'s fundamental disposition that the change has taken place, the change whereby he is persuaded

[1] Kierkegaard, *Concluding Unscientific Postscript*, trans. Swenson and Lowrie (Princeton, 1944), p. 221.

of good will not only in the castle but in everyone around him. He cannot be said to have deserved the transformation or to have wrested it from the castle by his own efforts. It has simply come about in the way described, and there must always remain some mystery about why it should have happened.

Kafka observed to a friend, 'Edschmid maintains that I smuggle miracles into ordinary events. Of course that is a serious mistake on his part. Ordinary events are a miracle in themselves. I only write them down. Maybe I illuminate things a little too, like a projectionist on a half-darkened stage. But that's not right. In reality the stage isn't dark at all. It's full of daylight. That's why people close their eyes and see so little.'[1]

K. is in just such a position where he sees the stage full of daylight. But what word are we to use, to epitomize the whole process by which this has come about? If someone asks what *The Castle* is about, how can we tell him briefly, without entering on a prolonged commentary? I suggest that the answer should be—it is a novel about a man's entry into a state of grace. By this I do not mean to imply that any of us has superior knowledge of what states of grace are 'really' like. I mean that it lies within the normal meaning of these words to apply them to K.'s condition. In this sense it can be freely said that the castle in this novel is the 'seat of grace', so long as that is not taken to imply that we are in a position to compare the seat of grace with the castle and establish an

[1] G. Janouch, *Gespräche mit Kafka* (Frankfurt, 1951), p. 38.

identity. We are too often bedevilled by the notion that when a statement such as Max Brod's is made an ultimate comparison of this kind is intended. How could it be, since one half of the parallel is by definition beyond human comprehension? We have as little right, or as much, to interpret Kafka's castle in this way as we have with Bunyan's Celestial City or Wolfram von Eschenbach's Holy Grail, or any other of the poets' concrete representations of invisible things. There is no *more* reason to describe them briefly in religious terms than in any others. Nevertheless, to deny any quality of grace in K. on the grounds that grace must always remain unrecognizable is to expect words to mean more than, in the nature of things, they ever can mean.

If the hypothetical questioner asked further what was meant by 'a man's entry into grace', the answer might be expanded. In this novel, it might be said, a man is desperately searching for some external confirmation of his private judgment which will bring him certainty. He struggles on until, realizing the hopelessness of it all, he gives up all expectation. Whereupon, from having been filled with distrust, malice, hatred, yearning, dissatisfaction, introspection (for all that he had some likeable aspects too), he becomes certain, sympathetic, charitable, forgiving, self-forgetful. All this has taken place in relationship with a castle, whose activities can be interpreted, with good will, as a series of unrecognized benevolent aids to K. on his path. (This has already become partly apparent—further indications of it must be reserved till later.) The castle is not itself a final authority, to be sure: it belongs to a Count, and we are free to imagine ducal, regal and imperial palaces beyond it. But this is how things are in reality. We are not confronted with a throne of grace whose presence can be demonstrated with logical finality. We are using the word 'grace' here to mean just such a relationship as exists in reality and in this novel. K. has done nothing to deserve his transformation, it is quite gratuitous. So long as he demanded his rights he got his deserts. But there was nothing he could do about it; he was not in a position to make any conscious choice and could only wait. So long as he imagined that his goal was in the castle or beyond, he waited against his will. The moment he gave up completely, a miracle transformed his reality. This, it would have to be explained, is what is meant here by the action of grace.

There are certain distinctions to be drawn between this and what certain theologians such as Karl Barth have described as grace, although there is a basic similarity. K. does not show obedience, at least not to the command issued to him by Erlanger. Nor can his transformation be described as specifically Christian, though there are theologians who would claim all such metamorphoses for Christ. There is nothing explicit in this novel that fits precisely with Barth's definition of grace: 'Grace is the incomprehensible fact that God is well pleased with a man, and that a man can rejoice in God. Only when grace is recognized to be incomprehensible is it grace. Grace exists, therefore, only where the Resurrection is reflected. Grace is the gift of Christ, who exposes the gulf which separates God and man, and by exposing it, bridges it.'[1]

The work of Christ here is something that can be believed, but it does not seem to have been Kafka's intention to imply that.[2] Indeed, treating as he does of a man who achieves certainty through unawareness, he has no machinery for expressing such belief. To use such a term as grace is thus not to remove doubt or belief. There is always the infinite sceptic to recall the castle's possibly inferior rank in the hierarchy, there is the literary critic's reminder that the castle is in itself a fiction, and the psycho-analyst's offer of a quite different explanation. But this kind of doubt, and the beliefs which go with it, are concomitants of the search for knowledge, as distinct from K.'s existence in unawareness.

In any case, greater achievements than K.'s are recorded in this novel. I mean the achievements of Frieda, Gardena and Olga.

---

[1] Karl Barth, *The Epistle to the Romans* (London, 1933), p. 31.
[2] Nor do I want to say that Christians alone are capable of having such experience. But this is not the place to compare Christianity with other religions.

VI

'It was she who first gave me the idea that a person does not (as I had imagined) stand motionless and clear before our eyes with his merits, his defects, his plans, his intentions with regard to ourselves exposed on his surface ... but is a shadow, which we can never succeed in penetrating, of which there can be no such thing as direct knowledge, with respect to which we form countless beliefs, based upon his words and sometimes upon his actions, though neither words nor actions can give us anything but inadequate and as it proves contradictory information — a shadow behind which we can alternately imagine, with equal justification, that there burns the flame of hatred and of love.'[1]

It is time now to stop seeing the novel through K.'s eyes and to look for those inter-relationships and significances which he, being part of the story, is unable to perceive. K. is never in a position to reflect, for example, on the sequence of events in the final chapters, where he is first abandoned by his assistants, their work being apparently done, then summoned to Erlanger and, having withstood temptation, feels in harmony with the officials. A document has been torn up, a victory seemingly celebrated, and K. is content to imagine Klamm in the most loving relationship with Frieda. It is not K.'s business to inquire into the meaning of all this. Yet it is not unreasonable for an outsider to assume a pattern unifying these

[1] Proust, quoted by John Wisdom, *Other Minds*, p. 192.

apparently unconnected events. With good will towards the castle, the pattern is clear—K. has been
persuaded of his insignificance, his humility has been
subjected to an exacting test, and his endurance is
rewarded. It may at least be so, and while it would
be presumptuous for K. to claim it, it is less presumptuous in a reader. Adopting, then, a more well-
disposed point of view towards the castle and to K.'s
environment in general, what picture emerges?

To take a point at random, there is Klamm's second
letter to K., which he regarded at the time with such
suspicion:

'To the Land-surveyor at the Bridge Inn. The land-
surveying you have carried out so far meets with my
approval. The work of your assistants is also praiseworthy, you manage to keep them hard at it. Do not
slacken in your zeal. Continue your work to a good
conclusion. Any interruption would make me em-
bittered. For the rest, be of good cheer, the question
of wages will be decided shortly. I am keeping you
in mind' (p. 142).

In the light of the reward K. does receive at the
end, this makes much better sense. Casuistry is needed
to interpret K.'s spying out the land as surveying, and
this must be accounted a fault, from the present point
of view. Apart from that, the letter is straightforward.
As with the first letter from Klamm, it is in the main
K.'s unquiet conscience ('an unquiet, not a bad one')
that hinders him from trusting Klamm's word. He
rejects the assurance because the castle merely insists
that he knows enough already. The fact that in the

first letter the words 'as you know' are added to the statement destroys its value in his eyes. Given a quiet conscience he need have troubled no further.

Almost from the outset, K. is encouraged to see events and people in a friendlier guise. It is not a simple matter, however, to ascribe good motives, and may need passionate determination as well as trust. Frieda indicates this to K. when she says 'If only you knew, with what passion I search for a grain of goodness for myself in everything you do and say, even if it hurts me' (p. 188). His fashion of interpretation is a matter of his disposition, as hers is; things are to him as he is disposed to see them. He can at least recognize this, though he cannot himself change his disposition. That, at least, is how both villagers and castle present the situation to him from the first day of his stay.

The choice between sympathy and hostility, trust and suspicion, is first presented to K. by the carrier Gerstäcker, who offers to drive him back to the Bridge Inn after his brief visit to the laundry in Lasemann's house. K. is puzzled by this act of kindness, which he imagines to be in conflict with the strict ordinances of the castle, and calls out after a while to ask whether Gerstäcker has permission to drive him around on his own responsibility. Receiving no answer he throws a snowball full in the man's ear. This brings Gerstäcker to a halt, but although he makes no reply, the sight of his wretched face compels K. to put his question in a different tone of voice. 'What he had said before out of spite he now had to repeat out of sympathy' (p. 28). This time he asks whether Gerstäcker will not be punished for giving him a lift. Gerstäcker's answer ends the first chapter on a note of choice: '"What do you want?" ['Was willst du?'] asked Gerstäcker uncomprehendingly, but awaited no further explanation, called to his horses, and they drove on' (p. 28).

From K.'s point of view, Gerstäcker simply does not understand what K.'s question means. The phrase 'Was willst du?' implies, like the French 'Que veux-tu?', some weary resignation. At the same time it can be read as asking 'What do you want? Do you choose that I shall be punished or not? Will you put the question in spite or in sympathy?' The fact is that Gerstäcker has already suffered for his action, not as the result of any intervention by the castle but at K.'s own hands. The question asked in spite carries its own punishment. A good deal of the real or imagined hostility towards K. arises similarly from the assertiveness or presumptuousness of the villagers; when he suffers, as he does at the hands of Gisa, the castle has no hand in it. Indeed the castle bell has just rung out in its ambiguous fashion (as it seems to K.), 'with rhythmic gaiety' and 'painfully too': it can be heard in both ways, and there is a second bell for those who will make no choice at all, a 'weak and monotonous chime' that seems to K. at this stage to suit the weary journey through the village (p. 27). There is nothing pure, certain or unchangeable about it as yet.

Shortly afterwards Gerstäcker's question is repeated to K. by an official at the castle. When K. has explained (though falsely) his situation and desires

86

over the telephone, the answer comes 'Was willst du?'
There is no possibility of weary resignation in the
words this time, it is a direct question. But K. scarcely
hears it; convinced that nothing can come of this
conversation he makes an insincere inquiry and
hangs up. A little later, he sees the fact of choice quite
consciously. Looking at Klamm's letter, 'he saw in
it . . . an open choice presented to him; it was left to
him to make what he wanted of the orders in the
letter' (p. 36). But the recognition of the fact cannot
alter the choice he does make. He is disposed towards
suspicion and acts accordingly.

For a great part of the novel K. realizes the good
intentions of others almost against his will. The
schoolmaster strikes him at once as 'a really domineering little man', and K. fancies he is flattered by
his position of authority and the attentiveness of his
pupils. Yet the schoolmaster's first words are 'more
mild' (or 'more meek'–'sanftmütiger') 'than K. had
expected' (p. 20). A little later, when Gerstäcker
offers to take K. home, K. feels that 'the whole scene
did not give an impression of particular friendliness'
(p. 26), although he has been treated in a 'not unfriendly' fashion for the last hour or so. Similarly,
in his conversation with the hostess at the Bridge Inn,
the woman's laughter sounds 'mocking, but much
more gentle than K. had expected' (p. 69). K.'s
expectation is disappointed in this way on other
occasions. He is unwilling to be persuaded that he
has 'a host of good friends at the castle', and treats
the suggestion with mockery. Not until after the

horrifying experience of freedom and isolation in the Herrenhof courtyard is it said of K. himself that he had 'grown more mild' (p. 147).

All this is a matter of K.'s mood. In saying that the villagers and the castle are hostile, dictatorial, well-disposed or acting in K.'s best interests, one is saying that they appear so to him. Yet the mere fact that he has an inkling of their good will, even when on the whole he expects only hostility from them, is an indication that in his transformed mood at the end he might be prepared to reflect on his past experiences differently. And since we are now taking a bird's-eye view denied to K. it may become possible to observe significances of which K. is oblivious.

An episode where, if K.'s limited viewpoint is adopted, there is a sense of frustration and meaninglessness, whereas from the general viewpoint there is possible meaning, is that in Lasemann's house (pp. 19-26). This follows immediately on K.'s first and only attempt to reach the castle on foot; utterly exhausted, he leaves the 'straitening street' ('die festhaltende Strasse') for a narrow alleyway. Seeing a house, he enters and finds himself in a room filled with smoke and steam, surrounded by people who seem not particularly pleased to see him. He is told to sit down, water is splashed in his face, and since nobody takes any further notice of him he falls asleep. Nevertheless, on waking, he offers thanks for hospitality, only to be more or less dragged to the door and sent out into the snow again. From K.'s point of view the whole affair looks rude, inconsequential and inhospitable. There is, however, another aspect of which even he seems partially aware. He cannot be wholly aware of it since he cannot know the pattern of events later in the book. K. arrives at the house, as he arrives for the Bürgel interview, at a moment when he has at least temporarily given up hope of entering the castle. The sight of the house he interprets as a sign that he is 'not abandoned'. And there *are* suggestions, at least to begin with, that the inhabitants are well disposed towards him: a 'friendly' peasant welcomes him in, and a woman's hand reaches out to save him from stumbling. Thus far there is normality. Inside, the scene has more of a dream-like quality. In the rolling smoke and steam K. stands 'as though in clouds'. Not, it should be noted, in 'clouds of steam', not the usual metaphor, but as though he were actually standing in clouds, as if he were taken out of his earthbound existence. A voice then calls to K. asking who he is, and the narrator's comment on his reply again has overtones of meaning. '"I am the Count's land-surveyor", said K., and sought thus to justify himself before the still invisible ones' ('und suchte sich so vor den noch immer Unsichtbaren zu verantworten'). Why should these villagers be described as 'invisible ones', instead of by the more normal phrase, 'these invisible people?' A vague sense of mystery is conjured up by these words. The mystery increases when K.'s attention is suddenly caught by the sight of a woman suckling a child in the corner. This is the woman whose appearance has already been described, and which suggests indistinctly the figure of the Virgin in some Nativity scene. K. himself finds her surprising, though he is unable to say wherein the surprising element consists. For the reader, there comes a feeling that the scene is of some importance for K., though he too is unable to say why. The girl seems to preside over the scene–K.'s attention is repeatedly drawn to her, and before he leaves he actually jumps round so as to face her. As soon as he does so, however, he is dragged away by a man at each elbow, much as he is dragged away later from the officials' corridor by the landlord and his wife. Has all this any recognizable significance?

Scarcely–it remains for the most part a mystery. But as K. leaves there is a small incident, for which no explanation is given, but which seems more readily placeable.

'All this had lasted only a minute, and at once K. had one of the men to right and left of him and was being dragged by them, as though there were no other means of making themselves understood, silently but with all their strength towards the door. The old man was delighted over something in all this, and clapped his hands. The washerwoman too started laughing, and the children suddenly shouted like mad' (p. 24).

Is this applause for K., or are they delighted to see the last of him? K. in his present mood would be more likely to assume the latter, though once again he is too weary to speculate about it. Yet the same question of dual interpretation arose after the Bürgel interview, when the bells seemed to proclaim a joyous victory, while the landlord heard them expressing exasperated anger. It may well be applause here; the peasants have been by no means unfriendly towards K., and there is a sense in which he seems to have benefited by his stay in the house. He is refreshed, he moves 'more freely' than before, and when he arrives outside the scene seems 'a little brighter'. He has also become 'rather more sharp of hearing', as though he were better able to interpret what he hears than formerly. It is conceivable that K. has been present at some strange ceremony of whose meaning he has been only dimly aware through the impressive figure of the girl, and that the clapping of the old man, the laughter of the woman, the shouting of the children was a rejoicing at its happy conclusion. The fact that K. is not allowed to remain does not contradict this—he is, as one of the villagers observes, an exceptional case, whereas they are content to remain where they are. The mystery that still envelops the scene is of the kind that must accompany any supposed contact with spiritual forces.

Kafka's style always compels the reader to adopt first the standpoint of the character whose story is related, since only the reflections of this character are actually recorded. The rest is related without causal or logical connection. Friedrich Beissner has observed this effect in Kafka's story *Die Verwandlung*, in which Gregor Samsa is transformed into a repulsive insect. Since only Samsa's account is given, the reader is gradually forced into accepting it. Beissner recalls however that in an early edition Samsa was portrayed in a text-illustration as a man, suggesting that to all outward appearance he remained one. Similarly, K.'s subjective experience here is not solely valid. From the villagers' point of view, this episode in Lasemann's house may have represented K.'s first acceptance by the castle, to be confirmed almost at once by the arrival of the two assistants.

The actions of the castle are often perceived thus dimly in the background, being related to the events in the narrative much as the text-illustration is related to the story of *Die Verwandlung*. They are not openly asserted because of the limitation of the narrator to K.'s position. The task of a reader at his second reading is to inquire what other interpretation may be placed on the events other than that presented to him through the eyes of K. Thereupon the contours of the castle are perceived surrounding the story like the air round an open hand. The difficulty lies in forcing one's gaze away from the hand and concentrating it on the enveloping insubstantiality. This is of course the difficulty with all religious or metaphysical thought, but to imagine the hand without the air about it is even more difficult.

VII

It has already become apparent that there are one or two features of the Lasemann episode which correspond to those of the Bürgel interview. Both take place at a moment when K. has given up the attempt to reach the castle; in both, K. makes some progress towards freedom–though vastly more in the interview than in Lasemann's house; on each occasion K. falls asleep at the crucial moment and is ignorant of what is happening. On awakening, he is treated with brusqueness and finally ejected, although this is accompanied by sounds which might be taken for applause and rejoicing. It is as though the castle were only able or willing to assist K. when he feels himself utterly helpless, although once its help has become acceptable there is pleasure. These, however, are not the only 'victories' in the novel.

The castle is concerned not only with K., but also with others of a similar disposition, whose progress is just discernible through K.'s eyes. K.'s meetings with Frieda and the hostess at the Bridge Inn, like the episode at Lasemann's house, have certain features in common with the Bürgel interview. They scarcely amount to a repetitive pattern. It is rather a question of motifs, images, situations in the interview which are taken up and repeated in a recognizably related sequence. One point has to be observed, however,

in drawing these analogies. It is that Frieda and the
hostess may well be—indeed K. says of Frieda that
she is—further advanced in their relationships with
the castle than K. ever is. Both women have enjoyed
the love of Klamm, and thus presumably have known
something like K.'s final experience. But they have
returned to the normal life of the village, where they
continue their everyday affairs. In their meetings with
K., however, K. stands in relationship to them as
Bürgel does to him. There is a mutual involvement
whereby each furthers the other. Seen in this light,
the experiences of Frieda and the hostess continue
the story from where K.'s leaves off.

At the first sight of Frieda, K. is struck by the look
in her eyes, a look of 'remarkable superiority'. 'When
her gaze fell on K., it seemed to him that it had accomplished things that concerned him too, things of
whose presence he knew nothing yet, but of whose
presence the glance convinced him' (p. 49).

There is 'something gay and free about her' (p. 55)
which K. observes only after he has been with her
a while. She is in fact accustomed to being in Klamm's
presence, and her position is one that carries with it
some esteem. All the same, she seems as anxious for
a meeting with K. as Bürgel proves to be later. She
seems to accept K.'s suggestion that she has not yet
reached any final goal, and that a man even of his own
stature is able to afford her help. 'Your eyes, don't
laugh at me Fräulein Frieda, speak not so much of a
past as of a future struggle. But the opposition of the
world is great, and grows greater with greater goals,

94

and there is no disgrace in securing the aid even of a little man with no influence, who is struggling in the same way' (p. 52).

It is Frieda who demands to see K. alone, and deceives the landlord into thinking that the room is empty; she begins their love-making, and at the end it is she, not K., who is heartily embraced and congratulated, as though she had performed some praiseworthy deed. It is hard to see why these congratulations should follow on this love-making unless it is that Frieda has prospered in some way by the encounter as K. prospered by the meeting with Bürgel.

There are parallels between the two scenes, some very slight, some more striking. K. is hiding in fear when Frieda enters the bar, just as Bürgel hides when K. enters his bedroom. From his hiding-place, K. is able to touch Frieda's foot as she fends off the curiosity of the landlord, an action which brings him a sense of security; similarly Bürgel allows K. to hold his foot when he is at his lowest ebb, as though this too might strengthen him. (Is there some fetishism here?) Once Frieda and K. are left alone, however, her actions become disconcertingly rapid: 'The landlord could scarcely have left the room when Frieda turned out the electric light, and was with K. under the bar-counter. "My darling! My sweet darling!" she whispered, but without touching K. at all; as though faint with love she lay on her back with arms outstretched, time must have been unending for her happy love, she moaned rather than sang some little song' (p. 55).

No word of love has passed between Frieda and

95

K. No explanation is offered for her sudden protestation or for her extreme happiness in K.'s presence. Seen through K.'s eyes these words and actions must be either bewildering or flattering. But are Frieda's endearments meant for K. at all? She is Klamm's beloved, not K's: why should her words not be addressed to him? Here is just one of those scenes where the invisible fills in the contours of Frieda's embrace. Of course it may not be so. Frieda's words with which she turns at length to K. and clutches at his body are capable of different interpretations. When she says 'Come on, it's stifling down here' she may mean merely the atmosphere under the bar. Her actions can be ascribed either to sudden lust or to desperation at her removal from Klamm's company. She may in fact be taking leave of Klamm in order to dissuade K. from his presumptuous plan of entering the castle. Only the compulsion on the reader to see things as K. sees them makes her words seem to be addressed to him.

Frieda's bodily attitude here is one which is repeated like a motif through all the scenes I am describing. K. too lies prostrate with outstretched arms as he finally falls asleep on Bürgel's bed; the hostess too momentarily takes up this position as though it were a secret sign. It recurs again at an important moment in the scene in the Herrenhof courtyard.

The night passes in fierce love among the beer-puddles. For K. it brings no release, only a feeling of estrangement and isolation, a foretaste of what he is to feel after waiting in vain for Klamm. At length, just as K. is summoned later by the voice of Erlanger in the adjoining room, so Frieda is called for now by Klamm behind the intervening door. And as K. at first hesitates to go, and is urged on by Bürgel, so now Frieda holds back, and is urged on by K. There is this difference, that K. finally accepts, from sheer weariness, whereas Frieda determinedly refuses. Nevertheless the conclusion of the scene is still related in pattern. When K. is dragged away from the corridor, in the later scene, the doors open one after another and a stream of officials throngs behind his back: communication is established once again after the long period of isolation. Frieda's 'victory', if it is one, is signalled in similar fashion. After Klamm has at length been brought to silence by her refusal 'the door to the courtyard was opened, the peasants and Olga, whom K. had quite forgotten, came streaming in' (p. 57). This irruption of society is repeated with greater emphasis at the end of K.'s meeting with the hostess. It seems to be part of the rounding off of such scenes. Finally, the congratulations and rejoicings are not omitted, though here they are quite unambiguous. When K. and Frieda return to the Bridge Inn, the hostess comes up on purpose to see her: 'Frieda called her "little mother", there was an incomprehensibly warm greeting with kisses and long embraces' (p. 58).

K. observes that something has been accomplished without knowing what. At the last, however, in his conversation with Pepi, he imagines he has gained some insight into Frieda's motives. '"Selfish?" [he

replies to Pepi] "you might say rather that by sacri-
ficing what she had and what she had cause to expect
she has given us both the opportunity to prove our
worth in a higher post"' (p. 355). This is said from
K.'s new, well-disposed point of view. But if it was
indeed Frieda's purpose to forgo the love of Klamm
in order to prompt K.'s willingness to remain in the
village, the rejoicing when her first step has been
accomplished is easier to understand. For Frieda does
not suppose that she has thereby run counter to
Klamm's wishes. Her first instincts are to be regretful;
later, however, the night becomes a precious memory.
It was, she believes, Klamm himself who brought
them together: 'blessed, not accursed, be that hour'.
Thus in abandoning the bliss of Klamm's presence,
Frieda carries out his further purposes, as indeed K.
himself is left at the end with Pepi, for whose sake
he is willing to abandon his new-found freedom.
There is no finality anywhere in these lives except that
of realizing that the castle cannot be entered. On the contrary there is constant renewal of conflict with the 'opposition of the world' and with selfish mistrust of love.

An attitude of good will is the only one which
comes anywhere near making sense of Frieda's actions; without this it is impossible to reconcile her
apparent lust for K., her defiance of Klamm, the
impression of spiritual superiority which she makes
on K., and the detailed incidents of the scene just
described. Speaking of Frieda later, however, K.
makes a remark suggesting that Frieda too has her
superiors. '"Have you ever noticed her look?" [he

asks] "It wasn't the look of a barmaid any longer, it was almost the look of a hostess. She saw everything, and each individual at the same time, and the look she had for the individual was strong enough to subdue him completely"' (p. 353).

This is at the end, when Frieda's task for K. has been successfully accomplished. It suggests not only that Frieda too has progressed during the course of the novel (there seems to be a slightly ludicrous advancement in rank from barmaid to hostess) but also that, in the strange hierarchy of the village, promotion goes with spiritual stature and depth of insight. This kind of stature is commonly described by K. in terms of the look in the eyes and the general physical impression. It is time now to see what impression he does in fact have of the hostess.

The hostess at the Bridge Inn, Gardena by name, is the most authoritative and impressive person that K. meets in all his course. None of the officials affect him as she does, not even Klamm, and she is only less terrifying than the hostess at the Herrenhof, the principal inn of the village. At his first encounter with her she appears as 'a giant figure, almost darkening the room'. When K. presses his claim to speak personally with Klamm, she grows terrible: 'it was frightening to see her sitting now more upright, her powerful knees ['die mächtigen Knie'] thrust forward through the thin frock' (p. 63). A likeness of her can be seen in some of the statues of Henry Moore.[1] One

[1] I am thinking particularly of the *Reclining Figure* for the Time and Life Building, exhibited at Holland Park, London, in 1954.

word in particular that is used to describe her—the word 'mächtig': 'powerful' or 'mighty'—attracts attention. It is used sparingly in the novel, but always consistently. Thus the Bridge Inn landlord seems to K. to be applying it indiscriminately. '"Get along," said K., "you think everyone is mighty. Me too, I suppose?" "You," he said, shyly but seriously, "No, I don't think you are mighty"' (p. 17). The word is reserved for only a few characters in the novel, for a minor official, for the schoolmaster, and Barnabas. Klamm is referred to more than once, not with the simple adjective, but as 'ein Mächtiger', one possessed of might. But of all the villagers it is Gardena to whom the word is most frequently applied. She is K.'s 'mighty enemy' (p. 185); and his first impression of her as he arrives at the inn is even more imposing than the sight of Frieda: 'filling the doorway stood the mighty figure of the hostess' (p. 13). This may go some way to explaining why Gardena embraced Frieda with such fervour after her night with K. She greets her as one pursuing the same path as herself.

Gardena was Klamm's beloved long before Frieda was. But like Frieda, she lost the happiness of his company, and entered the normal life of the village as wife of the Bridge Inn landlord. Her story continues Frieda's, as it were: it narrates the course of a life still devoted in memory to Klamm, but confronted with a world which has small understanding of what that devotion means to her. Her husband is a good-natured, pipe-smoking publican, with no concern in her other affairs; Klamm has not shown by word or glance that he has any recollection of her presence; she is resigned to the belief that she is completely abandoned by him. Yet unlike Amalia, who refused her summons to an official, Gardena is transformed by her memories of Klamm, the moment that they touch her mind and heart strongly; she then appears 'much younger', and 'all suffering seems to be removed from her' (p. 95). To have been Klamm's beloved is not enough in itself. Afterwards comes the need to believe in him and his good grace even when he appears totally remote and oblivious.

For these reasons, no doubt, Gardena seems to be as anxious to meet K. as Bürgel is, and when they do meet, it is in similar circumstances, she lying in a very large bed, on the edge of which she, like Bürgel, invites K. to sit. The roles, however, are reversed, for it is not K. but Gardena on this occasion who is full of unknowing. Her part of the conversation is full of doubts, doubt that Klamm has any memory of her or that her life has any purpose pleasing in his eyes. K. on the other hand, and surprisingly enough at this stage, is much more full of confidence, at least confidence on her behalf. It is he who insists on interpreting all that has happened in a more favourable light. To have been Klamm's beloved, he observes, is 'an advancement in rank that can never be lost' (p. 103). He tries to persuade her that all her life since then has been governed by Klamm's will, and that she has every reason to continue in hope for herself and her family: 'Blessing was upon your head, but they [Gardena's husband and his relations] did not know how to bring it down upon themselves' (p. 104).

This assurance of Klamm's benevolence, so surprising in K.'s mouth, is perhaps what Gardena has been awaiting with such impatience. His more naïve acceptance counterbalances her doubt, is able to give her an assurance which she cannot gain by her own efforts, so that once again, as with Frieda, his relative inexperience prospers her. As K. gives his assurance, Gardena too lies 'outstretched on her back, gazing at the ceiling' (p. 104). Like Frieda, she is perhaps not thinking principally of K. now. And at once, K. suggests that the proper thing to do would be to ask Klamm: this, he suggests, would have brought down blessing on them all. The situation is just that of Bürgel inviting K. to put the question which would liberate them both and dissolve the whole oppressive structure of the castle. The blessing and the certainty await the expression of complete faith in Klamm. But once again the opportunity goes by; Gardena evades the point, and the pros and cons continue. Neither she nor K. is prepared to go so far, for what reasons one can only guess. Nevertheless, Gardena consents to listen more peacefully to K., and as their meeting concludes she seems to have gathered strength by it. She who had been lying weakly in bed, fighting for breath, now gets up and rushes into the kitchen to continue her everyday work. And once again, concluding the episode, a crowd of villagers enters the inn: 'When K. entered the dining-room, an astonishingly numerous company streamed in towards the tables, more than twenty people, men and women . . .' (p. 107). At the same time, a chorus of childrens' voices is heard in song, as though in repetition of the hand-clapping, the shouts, the ringing of bells and the embraces which conclude the other similar scenes. Seen through K.'s eyes, all this is explained by the hunger of the villagers whose meal has been delayed. Seen in relation to the other scenes, it suggests that there may be good cause for rejoicing in that Gardena has gathered strength.

The meetings with Frieda and Gardena are dimly echoed, as far as the pattern of motifs is concerned, in the episode at the Herrenhof courtyard. This time, however, the significance of the motifs seems reversed. K., at this point in his course, has none of the sub-missiveness to Klamm, or love for him, which the two women have. On the contrary, the main theme of the episode is K.'s determination to force Klamm into an interview face to face. For this reason, perhaps, whenever the motifs recur they seem to have a parodistic quality, rather than a positive meaning of their own. They have meaning by being contrasted with the parallel motifs in the other scenes.

K.'s intention is to use cunning. On first entering the Herrenhof inn on this occasion, he tries a ruse to gain entry into Klamm's room, pretending that Frieda has left a tablecloth there. Learning that Klamm is about to leave in any case, he tries the further ruse of entering Klamm's sleigh and waiting there to waylay Klamm when he does come out. This is, in its way, an attendance on Klamm akin to that of Frieda and Gardena. They too had waited for a sign from him, Frieda 'faint with love', so that 'time must have seemed unending', Gardena refreshed by his mere memory, so that 'all suffering seemed to be removed from her'. But they had not used any of K.'s wiles, at least not at this point in their lives, and their happiness is unmixed with any other feeling. K., for his part, also feels a kind of happiness as he waits in the sleigh, but it is luxuriating rather than blissful. Inside the closed vehicle he can yield to an almost sybaritic indulgence of the senses. There is a sweet flattering warmth, a mass of soft cushions invites him to recline at ease, the sleigh-driver provides him with cheap cognac which fills him with a sense of receiving praise and words of endearment. Yet at the same time he is uneasy, he has a slight awareness that this is not as it should be. 'The thought that in his present situation it would be better not to be seen by Klamm entered his consciousness only dimly, as a slight disturbance' (p. 125). Shortly afterwards, he is filled with greater uneasiness; he is 'reproachful towards himself', and when his happiness is suddenly disturbed he remarks with 'disquiet' the dripping of the cognac on the running-board. It is during these moments of semi-satisfaction that K. adopts the attitude of Frieda as she lay beside him outside Klamm's room: 'With outstretched arms, his head supported by ever convenient cushions, K. looked out of the sleigh towards the dark house' (p. 125). He awaits Klamm as Frieda awaited her beloved, but in snug and indolent expectation. The attitude or gesture recurs here vapidly.

Following on this comes, as in the meeting with Frieda and the interview with Bürgel, the summons to leave. This time it comes from a young official, who proves later to have been Momus, and who arouses consternation in K. The summons is, notably, not a rejection of K., but an order to go with the official since K. will fail to see Klamm whether he goes or remains. If K. were able to accede, he might still be received favourably, despite his attitude hitherto. But he refuses to obey, declaring that he prefers to miss Klamm by waiting rather than by leaving.

The close of this episode follows directly on K.'s 'non serviam'. It gains added significance by being associated with the events following on the scenes with Gardena and Bürgel. Whereas after these there came a streaming concourse of people, flooding in towards K., there is here a dreadful withdrawal. The official gives orders for the horses to be detached from Klamm's sleigh, and enters the house. In the remainder of the scene there is a steady retreat away from K.

'The sleigh-driver, submissive to the official but with an angry side-glance at K., now had to get down, in his fur coat, and began very hesitantly . . . to drive the horses with the sleigh backwards towards the wing-door. . . . K. found himself being left alone; on the one hand the sleigh was moving away, on the other, along the path K. had come, the young official —both indeed very slowly, as though they meant to show K. that it was still in his power to bring them back' (p. 128).

The retreat is long drawn out. At length the official enters the house, leaving the driver with the difficult task of driving the horses yet farther back into the stable. During the whole of this recession, the driver acts much as K.'s assistants do, in silent mimicry of K.'s own mood: 'quite taken up with himself, without any hope of driving off shortly . . . contemplating nothing at all but his own footsteps in the snow' (p. 129). K., he seems to imply, is similarly so taken up with the scrutiny of his past tracks, with recriminations and self-analyses, that he is not so much nearing his goal as letting it recede from him.

The contrast with the other scenes is in itself interesting. At the same time, the whole withdrawal seems to present what D. H. Lawrence styled 'the startling experience of mystic reversion'. It has quite a close parallel in a novel which has a good deal thematically in common with Kafka's *Castle*, Melville's *Moby Dick*. I am thinking in particular of the chapter in Melville's book entitled 'The Try-Works', which occurs just at the moment when the full implications of the pursuit of the whale strike Ishmael, rather as the implications of K.'s battle for the castle now strike him. In both cases there has been an attempt to gain victory over the mysterious enemy at all costs. In both cases there comes a turning-point when such a victory seems pointless. Throughout the 'Try-Works' chapter Melville contrives, as Kafka does, to present an atmosphere of sloth and indulgence. The try-works themselves, great vats for boiling down captured whales, and the dominant symbol of the passage, are the place where old sailors coil away for a nap, where the watch lounges on a 'sea-sofa'. At the same time, there is an atmosphere of self-devouring torture, for in the try-works the whale is boiled down with fuel from his own blubber. 'Like a plethoric burning martyr or a self-consuming misanthrope, once ignited, the whale supplies his own fuel and burns by his own body.' Having evoked over several pages this sugges-tion of comfortable ease, mock martyrdom, and introverted self-destruction, having allowed Ishmael to realize the mood if only vicariously, Melville introduces the sudden experience of recession: Ishmael, standing at the wheel, is suddenly aware of something fatally wrong. He can see no compass to steer by, only a jet gloom:

'Uppermost was the impression, that whatever swift, rushing thing I stood on was not so much bound to any haven ahead as rushing from all havens astern. A stark, bewildered feeling, as of death, came over me. Convulsively my hands grasped the tiller, but with the crazy conceit that the tiller was, somehow, in some enchanted way inverted. My God! What is the matter with me, thought I. Lo! in my brief sleep I had turned myself about and was fronting the ship's stern, with my back to her prow and the compass.'

The passage ends with a thunderous command to mankind not to trust the ghastly appearance of things seen in firelight but the 'golden, glad sun, the only true lamp—all others but liars'. Kafka's sober, unmagisterial narrative (though it is also more confined, less spirited, less concerned with the manly virtues) represents the same kind of experience. K.'s quest up to this point, like Captain Ahab's throughout his life, is essentially a self-enclosing one, only apparently directed towards an external goal, in fact driving reality farther and farther away from him. The recession from K. is a melancholy portrayal of his isolation, all the more striking when it is juxtaposed in memory beside the scenes of congratulation.

VIII

Evil has knowledge of good, good has no knowledge of evil.[1]

Frieda and Gardena may both be regarded as showing the possibilities of development inherent in K.'s story, the one voluntarily leaving a state of grace, the other longing for its return. There are two other women, whose lives show the effects of a refusal to obey orders issuing from the castle. They are Amalia and Olga, the younger and elder sisters of K.'s messenger Barnabas. The long chapter in which the history of their family is related presents the castle to K. in the worst possible light, and, as has been seen, fills him with punitive hatred for his two assistants. What relation have Olga and Amalia to the novel as a whole?

The main points of the story as K. hears it from Olga may be briefly recalled. Amalia, together with the rest of the Barnabas family, had attended a village festival during which an official, by name Sortini, was attracted by her unusual appearance. During the following night, he sent her a summons to appear instantly at the Herrenhof inn. Amalia, for reasons that are never explicitly given, tore up the summons and threw the pieces in the face of Sortini's messenger. Thereafter, the whole family came into disrepute in the eyes of the village, the father lost his position,

[1] Kafka, *Tagebücher, ed. cit.* p. 223.

he and the mother were struck down with rheuma-
tism, and since that day, while Amalia had devoted
herself to tending her parents, Olga and Barnabas
had tried every means in their power to re-establish
the family in the eyes of the castle.

This history has had some attention from theological
interpreters. Max Brod in particular has compared
it with the main theme of Kierkegaard's book, *Fear
and Trembling*. 'The Sortini episode is indeed a parallel
to Kierkegaard's book, which bases its argument on
the fact that God demanded an actual crime of
Abraham, the sacrifice of his child; this paradox
assists in reaching the triumphant conclusion that the
categories of morality and religion are not to be
imagined as in any way coinciding.' That is to say,
Sortini's command to Amalia is compared with God's
command to Abraham, the two commands typifying
the amorality of divine judgment when it is measured
by any human standards. I do not think, for my own
part, that the purport of Kierkegaard's book is
adequately expressed in this form: it seems to me
rather to aim at presenting a picture of Abraham as
a man who, like K. in the final chapters of *The Castle*,
is 'unaware' (with the distinction that Abraham consciously obeys, while K. does not). To quote an
entirely different point of view, however, Erich Heller
describes Max Brod's comparison as 'downright
blasphemy, and a critical insult to the intelligence of
a reader able to read for himself the Bible, Kierkegaard, and Kafka'.

'The comparison between Kierkegaard and Kafka

would indeed be relevant. It might bring home, even to a modern reader, the difference between Purgatory and Hell. For this is the precise relationship between Kierkegaard's *Fear and Trembling* and Kafka's *Castle*. The sacrifice of Isaac a parallel to Sortini's designs on Amalia? But this means, without any polemical exaggeration, to ascribe to the God of Abraham a personal interest in the boy Isaac, worthy rather of a Greek demi-god. Moreover, He, having tested Abraham's absolute obedience, did not accept the sacrifice. Yet Sortini (who conveys to Max Brod the idea of divine guidance and Heaven itself) can, to judge by the example of his colleagues, be relied upon not to have summoned Amalia to his bedroom merely to tell her that one does not do such a thing."[1]

Such are the difficulties into which argument by parallels tends to lead. Max Brod evidently cannot have meant to say: Abraham=Amalia, Sortini=God, Isaac=Amalia's virginity, and the substituted ram=a likely change of heart in Sortini. Literary analogies are more likely to be tangents than parallels. But Heller's main point is that the castle represents an obstruction in K.'s path rather than a symbol of his true destination, and Sortini's conduct here is the strongest card that can be played in support of such an idea.

On the other hand, the ambiguous nature of all the castle's actions needs to be taken into account. This ambiguous element is present also in the story of Abraham and Isaac, for it was evidently not God's

---

[1] Erich Heller, *The Disinherited Mind*, pp. 176-7.

intention, despite all appearances to the contrary, to make Abraham a criminal, but to test his faith. Is it possible to say that Sortini was similarly concerned to put Amalia's submissiveness to the proof? Erich Heller, judging by the example of Sortini's colleagues, rejects the idea. Yet there are few such examples to judge by. Apart from Sortini himself, the only official whose relationships with village women are described is Klamm, and there is nothing to indicate that he was not always most tender in their presence. Frieda herself, if Olga is to be believed, was summoned by Klamm in much the same fashion as Amalia was by Sortini (p. 227), yet K. imagines their meeting in the most innocent way. There is no observable scurrility in the officials as a body, though there is in some of their boorish servants: is Sortini an exception, does he represent that aspect of the castle which appears immoral, as it does to the village schoolmaster, or would he too have 'accepted the sacrifice'? The fact is, there is no means of making sure; since Amalia did not accept the command.

The question of immorality, distinct from the amorality to which Max Brod refers, still remains. Once again, there is a considerable amount of uncertainty. The story of Amalia's summons and her reception of it is related entirely through Olga, so that the reader never hears Amalia's own account and is never told the contents of the letter which caused such violent repulsion. There is in fact something sly about the narrative technique here, recalling the technique used for describing the wound in *A Country*

Doctor, where the words seem deliberately weighted to emphasize the worst aspects. A few words from Amalia about the letter would have made clear what its contents were, and either have constituted a direct indictment of the castle, or have revealed her as over-sensitive, or prurient. As it is, Olga, for her part, did not understand of the letter more than its general drift, and much of it remained incomprehensible to her since she was quite unacquainted with the words it used.

'The letter contained the most vulgar expressions, such as I had never heard before and could only half guess at through the context. Anyone who did not know Amalia and had only read this letter would have thought that a girl to whom anyone could write in such terms was dishonoured, even if she had not been touched at all. And it was not a love-letter, not a word of flattery in it. On the contrary, Sortini was evidently angry that the sight of Amalia had seized his attention and kept him away from his work' (p. 224).

The only words in the letter that Olga actually recalls are 'See that you come at once, or else.' All this naturally suggests immorality in any normal context, and not mere fornication but domineering lust. Yet as with Frieda's seduction of K. at the Herrenhof, the interpretation is open to doubt. Olga is presented as a witness without complete knowledge of the facts or even an adequate understanding of the letter, and even she does not accuse Sortini of immorality in so many words. What does emerge clearly from her account, without any reading between the lines, is that the letter was vulgar, peremptory, humiliating and affronting. And this is enough. The command to Amalia cannot be justified; it is no use pretending it was sweet and reasonable. Amalia's indignant rejection inevitably has one's sympathy: she is a human being with human feelings and the summons comes to her in a particularly repellent form. But this was also Kierkegaard's point: God's command to Abraham was not sweet and reasonable but an order to sacrifice his dearest possession. In this sense, the Sortini episode is a parallel, or rather has tangential reference to Kierkegaard's version of the Bible story. It represents in the acutest form the conflict between personal honour and the humiliations of submissiveness. As Camus observes, 'Être incapable de perdre son honneur pour Dieu, c'est se rendre indigne de sa grâce.'[1] There is no easy solution here in choosing between honour and grace. Certainly Amalia is not to be condemned for maintaining her self-respect.

To find any final answer to this question would be like finding an answer to the question of evil. All religions which assert the loving-kindness of God's purposes are confronted with an incongruity akin to that presented by the Sortini episode. If the castle is the seat of grace, how can Sortini be numbered among its officials? He might well stand for the object of Blake's line in the 'Tyger' poem: 'Did he who made the Lamb make thee?'

Some answer can be given, however, in terms of Kafka's novel, and in terms of Amalia's character.

[1] Albert Camus, *Le Mythe de Sisyphe*, p. 183.

Even in these terms it is not a final answer, for as K. says, 'whether she has been great or small, wise or foolish, heroic or cowardly, Amalia keeps her motives to herself, nobody will ever wring them from her' (p. 231). She does not stand motionless and clear before our eyes with her merits, her defects, her plans and intentions exposed on her surface. One can only record the impression which she makes on K.

Externally, Amalia has many marks of virtue. She is uncomplaining, hard-working, long-suffering, and her sincerity cannot possibly be doubted. She devotes most of her time to the care of her parents, who, as a result of her actions, have become incapable of looking after themselves. She takes upon herself moral responsibility for the whole family—'it is she who makes decisions in the family for good and evil; and of course she has to bear the good and evil more than anyone else' (p. 201). Her moral actions and moral decisions are not laid at anyone else's door. But with all this, her darkly drawn face makes an unpleasant impression on K.:

'From her resting-place she looked K. up and down as though in surprise at his still being there. Her gaze was as cold, clear, and steady as ever; it was not precisely levelled on what it observed, but passed—this was disturbing—just a little, almost imperceptibly, but indubitably beyond it. It seemed not to be weakness or embarrassment, nor dishonesty that caused this, but a continual desire, rising above all other feelings, for loneliness, a desire that perhaps even she was only conscious of in this way' (p. 197).

Amalia is cut off by this desire even from the physical objects in front of her, and not only from objects
but from people. It is difficult to believe that her
actions spring from really charitable concern. Her
kindness is selective, directed at her parents only, to
whom she owes a kind of debt; for Olga and Barnabas
she shows no concern whatever. 'She has no anxiety,'
Olga observes, 'neither for herself nor for others.'
She lives in a continuing exhaustion, doubt, and
sadness, which lends her a certain majesty, a nobility
of suffering. Yet the immediate effect of her presence
is oppressive: 'K. seemed to remember that he had
been concerned with her look on the very first
evening, indeed that the whole ugly impression this
family had at once made on him was due to this look,
which was not in itself ugly, but proud, and sincere
in its taciturnity' (p. 197).
Amalia's form of sincerity leads her to embrace
isolation and mute endurance with tenacity. Her
name, for what the information is worth, is derived
etymologically from a word meaning 'labour', and
she does labour in a world whose horizon stops at
her own eyeballs. By maintaining her self-respect she
is left with nothing but herself to respect, she is her
own judge. She resembles Abraham in one of the
several interpretations offered in Kierkegaard's book,
the Abraham who did not accept the command made
to him but resigned himself to the inhumanity of
God's ways—'his eyes were darkened and he knew
joy no more'. To say this is not to condemn Amalia
or to suppose her condemned. It is tragic, rather, to

observe that a refusal like hers, sincere and honourable as it surely must be, has led to this empty isolation. No one could have been more justified than she was, yet that very justification seems her undoing. She does not have the faith—and how should she?—to surrender her claim to be just, and throw herself on the mercy of an apparently voracious official.

Olga, her sister, stands in contrast to Amalia. Although equally involved in the disgrace which attaches to the whole of the Barnabas family, she has none of Amalia's rigid control. 'She seemed really happy to be able to sit with him here alone, but it was a peaceful happiness, certainly not at all troubled by jealousy. And this very remoteness from jealousy, and thereby from all severity, did K. good. He was glad to look into these blue eyes that were neither tempting nor imperious, but shyly resting, shyly holding their own' (p. 201).

Olga, unlike Frieda and Gardena, has never been Klamm's beloved. Nothing in her life has ever occurred to persuade her of good will in the officials. There have been no personal messages of encouragement addressed to her, no mementoes, no moments of superhuman conviction. On the contrary, she has been surrounded for the last three years or more by the hostility of the villagers and the indifference of the castle officials to the numerous appeals she has organized. Moreover, her thought is penetrating enough to accept no shallow answers; she is unable to take refuge in paradoxes. Yet Olga has more faith in the castle than anyone. Where Gardena was close to

despair because Klamm had given her no sign for
the past twenty years, Olga is still full of hope that
at length some sign of the castle's benevolence will
come. She is not concerned with her own justification,
but with the reinstating of 'our' good name, the
name of the Barnabas family, in the castle and village. It is she of all people who tells K. there is
no lack of love in the place, and that such a thing
as unhappy love is unknown in an official: 'There
is never any lack of love here ... We know that
women can do no other but love officials, once
the officials turn towards them, and in fact they
love them before that, however much they may deny
it' (p. 229).

She finds every reason for supposing Sortini to
have been genuinely in love with Amalia, emphasizing
his lack of worldly experience, the eagerness with which
he approached her at their first and only meeting, and
excusing the vulgarity of his letter. She suggests that
the sufferings of the Barnabas family may be due not
to the castle, but to themselves. She goes so far as to
take up sides with Frieda, whom on former occasions
she had decried, and against Amalia. Frieda, she
believes, was in the right to accept Klamm's command,
Amalia in the wrong to refuse: 'If I compare the two
cases, I am not saying they are the same: they are
related as white is to black, and Frieda is white. At
the worst one can laugh at Frieda, as I naughtily did
once in the taproom—I regretted it very much, later,
though even to laugh like that you need to be spiteful
or envious. At all events, one can laugh. But Amalia,

unless one is related to her by blood, can only be despised' (p. 227).

It is not a question of right and wrong here–K. soon finds distinctions, and reasons for defending Amalia– but of disposition. Olga does not criticize Amalia's conduct from lack of love, but because she is disposed to believe in the good will of the castle in the face of all denial. K. in his state of grace has no such obstacles to surmount as Olga has, he is simply unaware of the change in his disposition. But conceivably they do not even appear as obstacles to her. Her infinite doubt concerning the genuineness of Barnabas's relationships with the castle is matched with infinite faith that at each instant the castle's actions are consistent with love. And with this disposition, Olga seems to K. to be really happy. Her name is in fact derived from 'heilig', holy. Thus the two sisters, in some ways a Martha and Mary, present the outward marks of faith and distrusting resignation. As K. leaves them, he reflects on Olga's 'courage, her prudence, her intelligence, her sacrifice for her family. If he had to choose between Olga and Amalia it would not cost him much reflection' (p. 268). The change in his outlook is prepared by the encounter with Olga's tremendous faith.

The question of moral correctness is, then, never decided. The consequences of acceptance and refusal, as they appear to K., are delineated, while judgment is withheld. No arguments convince that Sortini was a moral man, filled with good intentions. There are rather the two attitudes, Olga's and Amalia's. Olga's peace of mind, however, owes nothing to glibness; it does not rest on paradox, as does the faith of the village elder, but on a strong belief that despite contradictions there is unique purity and love.[1]

Olga's narrative answers in advance the question raised by K.'s transformation in the final chapters: is it not inconsistent with human dignity to accept any grace which might conceivably come from such an institution as the castle? Without Olga it might be held that K. was treacherous in his sudden conviction that the officials are filled with joy and harmony. The point is put acutely once again by Albert Camus: 'K. . . . est à la fin du voyage un peu plus exilé puisque, cette fois, c'est à lui-même qu'il est infidèle et qu'il abandonne morale, logique et vérités de l'esprit pour essayer d'entrer, riche seulement de son espoir insensé, dans le désert de la grâce divine.'[2] But K., I suggest, does not *try* to enter such a state, he does enter it, and far from being a desert this Grace is portrayed in the novel as a source of peace, sympathy and happiness, even in the face of considerable tribulation. Nor is K. exiled at the end, but on much friendlier terms with those around him. Yet has not K. been unfaithful to himself? Is it not rather his human task to continue the Sisyphean struggle? The novel comes to a stop, with K.'s death dimly foreshadowed, before the question can be answered in respect to him. But the struggle has already been described in the account

[1] I should not be surprised, through this can only be a guess, if Olga and the Barnabas family were linked in Kafka's mind with the faith and history of the Jews.
[2] *Op. cit.* p. 183.

of Olga. Were K. to live longer, he might well encounter such tribulation as hers, and her attitude is
an indication of what his might become. There is
nothing dishonourable in Olga's conduct, she is
neither abjectly remorseful nor proudly resigned. Her
eyes are restful but they 'hold their own'. At the same
time, like the later K., her aim is not to take the castle
by storm or to force an interview face to face. She
continues to lead the life of the village with infinite faith.
'There is never any lack of love here.' She abandons
neither morality (for she is revolted by the thought
that Sortini's action *could* have been immoral) nor
logic (K. observes that she thinks with astonishing
clarity) nor truths of the spirit, unless truths of the
spirit exclude the possibility of loving-kindness. The
tragedy, that with all this there is not the remotest
sign of recognition from the castle—unless the appointment of Barnabas as messenger is so regarded—does
not deflect her faith in the slightest. It is not she who
is dishonourable, but the nagging voice of one's own
scepticism that seeks to interpret her motives in terms
of palliation and exculpation.

All this argument, however, only makes sense so
long as the castle and its officials are taken to represent
the relationships of men with the supernatural world.
The reader has to choose here too, between reading
the novel as a satire on bureaucracy or as a vast
metaphor, worked out to the last detail so that it can
stand as a whole and be experienced as a whole, a
metaphor of inward life. If the reference is taken to
be earthly and natural, Olga's faith in the castle can

only appear reprehensible, and K.'s private imaginings about the true nature of the officials have to be related to the conversion of Winston Smith, in Orwell's *1984*, to belief in the charitableness of Big Brother. This is what I meant when I said earlier that the pronouncements of theologians and totalitarian statesmen can sound alike. They can, but with this difference, that while it is dishonourable to submit to the will of men it is not dishonourable to submit to the will of God. Kafka's *Castle* makes positive sense only in so far as it is interpreted, and interpreted on theological lines. To remain content with sheer commentary, a purely literary approach, as I have tried to do in the main during this study, is part of a necessary scientific procedure, isolating the phenomenon. But when that has been done, and even while it is being done, it is not possible to leave the novel in isolation. All interpretation of motives is interpretation, not neutral commentary, and the only satisfying interpretations of conduct here are those based on theological considerations.

The same applies not only to the political but also to the psycho-analytical interpretations. At the very most, granted that the castle is meant as a mother-symbol and that the Count's permission is needed to possess her incestuously, psycho-analytical terms might be applied to K.'s quest. But they work far less smoothly in explaining why Frieda should give up the love of Klamm, or why Gardena, who has lost sight of him for so long, should appear so powerful, or why Olga, who has never seen Klamm, should have such faith. Once again, the satisfying answers are related to a view of the castle as a symbol concerned with transcendent reality. 'Satisfying', I realize, is a subjective term. But it needs pointing out that this commentary is influenced at every important moment by theological concepts. Where the commentary makes sense of the novel, it does so because it assumes that theological concepts are not empty formulas, but have reference to actual experience.

IX

Dumbness is one of the attributes of perfection.[1]

The Castle, like Kafka's two other novels, was never completed, and Kafka asked, before his death, that they should all three be destroyed. The history of editions of *The Castle*, which Max Brod so rightly published despite his friend's request, may moreover have led to some confusion. In the first edition, the last three chapters are omitted because they were felt to lead to no conclusion.[2] The form in which they appear in the second edition, ending with a half-promise by the hostess at the Herrenhof that she will summon K. to her next day, is still incomplete. In the third edition, published in 1946, they still appear in the same form, but with the addition, as part of Max Brod's epilogue, of the final page or so of manuscript, describing K.'s reluctant visit to the aged mother of Gerstäcker. This, written in a notebook which has further unfilled pages, breaks off in the middle of a sentence. It seems clear then that unless some part of the manuscript has still to come to light, Kafka was unable to round off what he had written. In addition, he seems to have felt that what was

[1] Kafka, *Tagebücher, ed. cit.* p. 224.
[2] The first edition, of 1926, includes the opening pages of chapter 18, but ends when Frieda abandons K. in order to tend Jeremiah – that is before the Bürgel interview.

complete should not be made public, although he did publish short stories during his lifetime.

These facts have some relevance to the present study. If the novel had reached so conclusive a point as I have implied, what prevented its conclusion? It is a common feature of Romantic writings that they remain fragmentary, but Kafka seems to have overcome his Romanticism, in the uncomplimentary sense of the word. He is not subjective, working off his neuroses, struggling towards identification with the universe, but has a wide and accurately stated view of many forms of human condition, an objectivity and generosity which, one would have supposed, would have allowed him to have overcome formal difficulties with relative ease. The mere fact that he can allow his *alter ego*, K., to be treated with such humour, or that he can set against him such figures as Frieda, Gardena, and Olga, is an indication of how far he was from being a harassed depictor of his own difficulties.

An ending for the novel was in fact envisaged. According to Max Brod's recollection of a conversation with Kafka, the end was to have shown K.'s final acceptance by the castle, an acceptance which Brod describes as 'ironically reduced to a minimum'. 'The supposed surveyor receives at least partial satisfaction. He does not give up his struggle, but dies of exhaustion. The villagers assemble round his death-bed, and at that moment the decision arrives from the castle; that K. has no legal right to stay in the village—but in view of certain accompanying circumstances he is allowed to live and work there.'[1] One would like to know how close this is to a verbatim account, and at what point in the composition of the novel, which extended over several years, this ending was conceived. It suggests a conception of K. as a man who, even at the end, is still trying to enter the castle, while the official decision suggests that all he could expect was permission to stay in the village. Yet in the final chapters as we have them, K. is no longer struggling, and is convinced 'to the point of being indifferent about it' that he will remain. The official confirmation of this can only be taken as ironical from the point of view that the castle must be entered at all costs. After the writing of the final chapters, I imagine, such an ending would no longer have been possible in quite that form.

The events of the last chapter may help the understanding of Kafka's difficulty. They are largely taken up with a long conversation between K. and Pepi, which may be briefly examined first, rather by way of parenthesis, though later events are not fully clear without it.

Pepi is of all characters in the novel the least sympathetic. Thanks to K., she believes, who enticed Frieda away from her position as barmaid, Pepi has been freed from her dark and narrow room downstairs, and has become a barmaid herself. She is full of the warmest flattery for K., her hero, her liberator. She is jealous of Frieda, fancies that she herself would have done far better as Klamm's beloved, asserts that

[1] *Das Schloss*, third edition, p. 415.

Frieda has connections with the castle 'that nobody knows about', so that no merit is due to her for her high position. She praises her own efficiency, expects to be loved by everybody, and foresees with chagrin her totally unmerited dismissal as soon as Frieda returns. She dreams of promotion beyond the rank of barmaid, of rising higher and higher in the hierarchy, of graciously inclining her ear to K.'s proffer of marriage, which he has not made, of nobly renouncing all her hard-won position and teaching him what true love means. In short, she presents all the unpleasantly egoistic aspects of K.'s quest, of which he has himself been aware from time to time, in a concentrated form.

Why should K. be plagued with all this nonsense at this juncture? Has it any significance in the pattern of the novel? It has, if one can imagine oneself in K.'s position for a moment, and realize that the characters in the novel do not always exist entirely in their own right but also to some extent as aspects of K. Here is K. now, established in the 'free' taproom, convinced he is going to remain, and dimly aware that at last he has 'good faith'. What more natural for him, seeing the kind of man he is, than to be tempted once again by dreams of grandeur? He himself is now where Frieda was, he can be jealous of her still higher position, fancy that he has at least got his foot on the bottom rung of the ladder, imagine himself in a position where he can preach to others on the nature of true love. With the realization of success comes the temptation to glory in it, which, as far as this kind of success is concerned, is to kill it on the spot.

Pepi presents obliquely the kind of egotism which might be imagined to arise in K. as a counterpart of the self-disregard in which he has been living for the past few hours. She expresses selfhood more completely than any other character. Her function is also, like that of several others, indicated by her name. Not that this interpreting by name has any value in itself: if the function is not clearly indicated in the character the name becomes an esoteric tag. But Pepi's name is in fact a commonly used abbreviation for Josef or Josefine, the name of K.'s counterpart Josef K. in *The Trial*, and the name given by K. as his own when he telephoned to the castle. She comes, as she often recalls, from 'down below', in a hidden, dark and narrow recess. One aspect of K.'s quest has always been the struggle for 'something vitally close, for himself' (p. 50). It is as though now, having failed to reach the castle, he suddenly finds this self looming up at him from the depths of unconsciousness, with all its comic evil revealed at last.

K.'s reply to Pepi presents the case for the castle and against attempts at bending it to one's own will. In doing this, K. manages both to preserve sympathy for Pepi and to indicate the relative nature of what he has achieved:

'It's just one job among others, but for you it's heaven itself, and so you take up everything with too much zeal, dress yourself up the way you think angels dress—but in reality they are different—you tremble for your job, feel you're being constantly persecuted, you try to win over by an excessive show of friendliness anyone you think could help you, and yet only offend them and repel them, because they want peace at the inn and not the barmaid's worries as well as their own' (p. 353).

K. could not put more clearly the different consequences of being desperately concerned to be in the right, and not minding. He does not distinguish himself from Pepi in these observations, imagining that for his own part he has the right answers, but treats both their cases as one and the same:

'I don't know if that's how it is, nor is my guilt at all clear to me, only when I compare myself with you there emerges some kind of notion that we have both toiled on too much, too noisily, too childishly, without enough experience, to get something which with Frieda's matter-of-factness and repose can be won easily and without fuss. We tried to win it by crying and scrabbling and dragging, like a child dragging at a table-cloth, gaining nothing but bringing down the whole gorgeous display and putting it out of its own reach for ever . . .' (p. 355).

Yet whatever Pepi may be, she is not a reflection of K.'s conscious self when he can answer her in this way.

The effect on Pepi is remarkable. She too becomes reconciled to her condition. In her last long speech to K. there is not a word that can be interpreted as spiteful, jealous, or self-seeking. She finds pleasure in the recollection of her life underground, speaks with kindness of her two room-mates, and abandons her ambitions in the taproom: 'It's warm and snug down there, and we press still closer to one another; no, although we have to make do with each other we haven't grown tired of each other; on the contrary, I almost like the idea of going back there when I think of my friends. Why should I get on better than they?' (p. 356). Her ideas are perhaps over-snug, but it remains clear that in the main K. has won her over to his way of thinking. He has brought about a funda-mental change in her disposition comparable to his own, the two of them are reconciled, and it does not much matter whether this reconciliation is thought of as between two different people or between two levels of consciousness.

In becoming reconciled with Pepi, however, K. is also reconciled to the idea of joining her in her narrow, dark, subterranean room. The end of his life is near, as is known from Max Brod's account of the intended conclusion, and Pepi has already spoken of her dismissal from the taproom as the closing of a grave over her head (p. 350). K. lets her go, with the promise to rejoin her in an hour. A reader may choose to read this as K.'s final acceptance of the fate pre-destined for him by the castle. He goes to his death reconciled. But he is not bound to Pepi's room for ever: 'There is no obligation on you, you will not always be bound to our room as we are' (p. 357). Despite the long and featureless winter down there the spring comes at intervals, Pepi observes, at which K. makes quick inquiry: 'How long is it then till spring?' He still has hope.

At this instant, the door of the taproom where K. and Pepi are talking is opened. 'Pepi shuddered in fright, having let her thoughts wander too far from the taproom, but it was not Frieda, it was the hostess' (p. 358). Had her thoughts remained in the freedom of the taproom she might not have feared the cessation of her brief life above ground. K., however, who shows no such fear, is left after Pepi's departure face to face with the hostess. She is not Gardena but the hostess at the Herrenhof, yet like Gardena she is a frightening figure with her bold reproofs and sharp commands, her sudden outbursts and challenges, and her dreaming eyes. There is also something about her that makes K. believe she is not only a hostess but also has 'some other purpose in mind' (p. 360). What else she is, K. never discovers. No explanation is given, and the conversation between her and K. is almost entirely concerned with the enormous size, the antiquity, and the unsuitability of the dresses in her wardrobe. With further revision by Kafka, some plainer hint might have been dropped. With a book as closely worked out as this it seems incredible that this conversation is meant to be as trivial as it looks. A suggested interpretation of the scene does at least, however, appear to provide an underlying sense and pattern. If the dresses are the disguises which the hostess is accustomed to wear when she announces to men the moment of their death, a good deal falls into place. It becomes clear why K. is so impressed by them, and why he says that they are more beautiful than any he has seen before. The hostess's irrepressible

cold shudder when they are mentioned is easier to
understand. So is the fact that on this occasion she
appears in a gorgeous evening-dress, and her remark
that her one aim is to dress herself ever more beauti-
fully. In fact, if this sense is taken, the novel may be
felt to end well enough without the addition of the
further pages of manuscript provided now by Max
Brod. The Charon-like figure of Gerstäcker already
has K. by the sleeve, to carry him away on his flat, seat-
less sledge. On the preceding page the hostess seemed
to be giving him instructions about K.'s destination.
And now the hostess concludes with the possibly
ambiguous remark: 'Tomorrow I shall be getting a
new dress; perhaps I shall send for you.' It at least
makes for an artistically rounded whole to suppose
that, while K. naturally cannot know it, with this
remark his story is as good as finished. But the suggestion does imply a degree of allegory such as is not
normally found in the rest of the novel, unless perhaps
in the Pepi episode.

At all events, the final lines recorded in Max Brod's
postcript may be felt to continue in the same mood.
There is the same scarcely definable atmosphere of
approaching death about the almost mythical figure
of the aged woman, who is Gerstäcker's mother: 'The
room in Gerstäcker's hut was lit only by a fire on the
hearth and the stump of a candle, in whose light someone was crouching in a niche beneath the jutting,
crooked roof-timbers, reading a book. It was Gerstäcker's mother. She gave K. her trembling hand and
told him to sit down beside her; she spoke with

difficulty, it was hard to understand her, but what she said . . .' (p. 427). Here the manuscript ends. What words this Norn-like figure might have uttered, what message she may have had for K., cannot be known. At the most there may be a feeling that K.'s end is now very near, and it is not difficult to imagine the concourse of villagers streaming in to surround his bed.

It may be that the novel was never finished because of the technical difficulty of maintaining the narrative from K.'s point of view up to the very moment of his death. Or Kafka may have lacked the courage or even the desire to go on analysing the final moments. Such reasons do not explain, however, why Kafka was opposed even to any publication of this novel. There is still a third possibility which would account for this too. It has already been seen how K. in his final moments is confronted by a sheer personification of egotism. May not Kafka, who after all must have been similar to K. in many ways, and who had managed to bring his protagonist to this point, have preferred not to expose himself to the vanity which publication, or even the prospect of publication after his death, might stimulate?

To judge by the fragments and variant readings published by Max Brod, Kafka seems to have contended with a strong desire to place the events of the final chapters a second time before the reader, in the worst possible light. One such fragment is that already referred to, mocking both at Bürgel and at K. for his credulity and self-importance after the interview. This

will not fit the novel on technical grounds, though
Max Brod does not say why he has excluded it from
the main body of the text. Yet the fragment does
indicate the difficulty Kafka had in permitting K. to
continue his relatively untroubled course. Similarly,
there is an alternative version of the final scene with
Gerstäcker. In the 'accepted' version, K. is on the
whole calm. There is slight hostility between him and
Gerstäcker, but at length they walk off together arm
in arm. In the variant, their hostility swells to a point
where they seem to be shouting abuse at each other,
and K. almost shows animosity:

'"I'm not going to share my secrets with you. You're
the one who swore at me when I was stuck outside
your door in the snow."

"But I did drive you to the Bridge Inn afterwards."

"That's true, and I never paid you. How much do
you want?"

"Have you got money to spare? Do they pay you
well at the school?"

"It's enough."

"I know a place where you'd be paid better."

"What, at your place, with the horses? No thanks."

"Who told you that?"

"You've been lurking around to catch me since
last night."

"There you're very much mistaken."

"If I'm mistaken, so much the better."'" (p. 428.)

Once again, Kafka seems to have been drawn
towards a less favourable depiction of K. which would
counterbalance the impression of the last chapters.

134

The lingering reluctance to present any suggestion of a 'happy ending' appears to have been overcome, as far as these events are concerned. Conceivably, however, this reluctance hindered any neat rounding-off of the work.

Kafka was very much taken with an anecdote about Dostoevsky, relating how the critics who first discovered his work were astonished at the purity and clarity of his vision, while he himself was full of doubt and remorse.[1] This, together with the last deleted passage quoted with aptness at the end of Max Brod's third edition, provides the best explanation of why Kafka neither completed this novel nor wished it to be published:

"You see things astonishingly well", said Olga, "sometimes you help me with a single word, it's probably because you come from abroad. But we, with our sad experiences and continual fears are frightened, without trying to defend ourselves, at a piece of wood cracking, and if one is startled, the rest are startled too, and can't even give the right reason. . . . How lucky it is for us that you came." For the first time K. heard here in the village an unconditional greeting, but for all that he had wanted it so much, and for all that Olga seemed so trustworthy, he was not glad to hear it. He had not come to bring anyone happiness; he was free to help of his own will, if occasion arose, but nobody should greet him as a bringer of happiness. Anyone who did that was drawing red herrings, requiring him to do things

[1] Cf. Kafka, *Briefe an Milena* (New York, 1952), pp. 17-19.

which, once forced in this way, he was not disposed for; with the best of good will on his part he could not do that. But Olga made up for her mistake when she went on: "Of course, when I fancy then that I might leave all my worries alone, since you would find an explanation and a way out for everything, you suddenly say something utterly, painfully wrong" (p. 429).

The mood which could delete this passage could delete the whole book.

A NOTE ON 'THE TRIAL'

I have decided to concentrate on only one of Kafka's full-length novels, though I have touched on several short stories and have quoted from his diaries and letters. There has been nothing so far about the other two novels, *America* and *The Trial*, though I hope both of them will appear differently in the light of what I have written. I do not in fact want to offer a complete commentary on Kafka's work, believing that literary criticism in general is already too voluminous. But I do want to indicate a possible way of reading Kafka; readers who find this way acceptable will be able to apply it for themselves to other works of his they read.

The Trial, for example, will be found to have much the same basic pattern as *The Castle*. It differs in so far as the question which concerns Josef K. is not whether he is accepted or refused, but whether he is innocent or guilty. But in attempting to reach a conclusion he is confronted by an organization of court officials very similar to that which operates from the castle; he is given the same kind of contradictory information by self-styled initiates, and entangled in the same web of doubts and certainties. In particular, it is noticeable how he is convinced from the outset that the court is hostile to him, corrupt, revengeful, senseless and incapable of human consideration. His denunciatory speech at his first examination, before he has had time to learn anything of the normal procedure, is an indication of his tendency to draw rash conclusions; it also prevents the examining magistrate from saying anything of importance, if he has anything of importance to say. Similarly, K. is told repeatedly that while he is certainly arrested, that does not in itself mean that he is accused, yet he begins to assume his own guilt as a necessary implication of his arrest. True, this assumption comes naturally when it is made by almost everyone else around him. Yet the official in charge of his arrest is explicit; 'I cannot tell you by any means that you are accused, or rather I do not know if you are. You are arrested, that is correct, I do not know more than that.' Much of K.'s terrible suffering is related to the unfavourable deductions he makes from simple facts.

Like the castle, the court reflects Josef K.'s moods and thoughts. Although he knows only approximately where it lies, it proves to be on the first staircase he chooses; the ruse he adopts, of pretending to be in search of a joiner called Lanz, is successful—the name Lanz seems to be accepted as a password into the courtroom itself; although no precise time is fixed for his appointment, he is reproved for coming an hour later than that which he had privately resolved to keep. The court, or its officials and associates, parodies his actions as the assistants in *The Castle* parody those of his namesake. Sometimes this parodying is in the nature of a forestalling of K.'s actions, or a silent reminder to him. Thus he complains to the court that its officials have 'defiled' the room of his neighbour, Fräulein Bürstner (in fact they have disturbed some of her photographs). It escapes his attention that on the evening of his arrest he himself, if anybody, defiled the room by exhibiting his lust for her body. Again, he sees a book on the courtroom table, containing a picture of a naked man and woman sitting together on an ottoman; he at once assumes that this is the kind of legal work normally studied by magistrates, is morally indignant and fails to notice that within a few moments he is close to being in such a position with a woman himself. Conceivably the picture was a dumb reflection of what was already in K.'s mind. (Or it may, of course, have been an incitement.) On another occasion, when he appears to admire the gloomy sunset pictures of the painter Titorelli he is offered not one but scores of copies of the same scene —an absurd exaggeration of his apparent preferences which does not, however, seem to strike him as comic.[1]

Yet with all this, there is never any evidence, apart from hearsay and rumour amongst those not in a position to know, that the court is hostile to K. On the contrary, both the guards entrusted with his arrest assure him of their friendly intentions, the typist and the usher at the court itself go out of their way to help him, and a presumably high official, the director of the chancellery, makes a special journey at night on his behalf. The episode of 'The Whipper', where the guards who arrested K. are flogged in his presence, will be felt to tell against any such picture of the court as a benevolent institution. Yet, as in the episode with Gerstäcker in *The Castle*, this punishment is a direct result of K.'s hostile frame of mind. It is he who

[1] 'You seem to like gloom', Titorelli observes.

has accused the guards of corruption, and the one action which might conceivably have released them —offering himself for punishment in their place—occurs to his mind only to be dismissed as impossible. Instead, he tries to bribe the whipper, to make him guilty of the very crime for which the innocent guards are being punished. This episode reflects not so much on the court as on K.'s mood. He would, he says, gladly flog the judges if he had the chance.

K. is not to blame for the course he adopts. What point is there in arresting him if he is not to be accused? And granted that deduction, why should he not try to discover the nature of the accusation and to justify himself? He does the natural thing in the circumstances. Nevertheless he does undergo towards the end a transformation comparable to the one in *The Castle;* his attitude towards his trial becomes entirely different. At first he is high-handed and independent, believing it to be his mission to introduce improvements in the legal system of the court. He believes his own trial to be specially complex and important, almost a test-case—if the court can be shown its folly in trying a man like himself, it may change its ways. He even imagines that others among the accused take him for one of the judges or magistrates, although this self-assurance proves hollow when he learns later that on the contrary they took him for a man already condemned. Above all he is convinced of his own innocence. That there are grounds for calling him licentious, uncharitable, jealous of his superiors at his office, suspicious, contemptuous and revengeful does not weigh against this in his mind. Only at the end when he is being led to his place of execution, does a brief glimpse of Fräulein Bürstner, whom he has treated with degrading lewdness, strike him with the force of a reproach. He follows her then 'not because he wanted to overtake her, not because he wanted to see her for as long as possible, but only in order not to forget the admonition which she represented for him'. But by this time he has already experienced a change of outlook. Gradually his early confidence has been undermined, first by the sudden sheer weariness which overtakes him (the parallel with *The Castle* is precise), then by the desire for outside assistance, and then by the wish to draw up documents in his own defence–a recognition that defence is needed. Paradoxically, the more firmly he proclaims his innocence the more concerned he is to establish it. Just as paradoxically, when Titorelli repeats continually that his very innocence is a point in his favour, he feels the more uneasy. He is caught in the dialectic of affirmation and denial: the pros and cons spin on endlessly.

The climax comes when K. decides to terminate the employment of his advocate, Huld (the name means 'Grace'). This looks like an act of desperation, and is comparable with the moment in *The Castle* when K. breaks off all communication with the officials. The chapter in *The Trial*, however, is not finished: a vital link in the story is missing. When it is taken up again, the emphasis has changed considerably. The scene is laid in a cathedral, a building whose Christian features are explicitly recalled by the lights symbolizing the

Trinity, the picture of the Entombment, the crucifixes, and the statue to the Virgin. There has not been hitherto in the novel any direct suggestion that the actions of the court have any connection with religious concepts. Yet at this point and in this setting K. hears for the first and only time a detailed explanation of his situation from an actual official of the court, the priest who styles himself the prison chaplain. Moreover, for the first time K. listens with respect and even a degree of affection to a court official. He has entered the church without thought of devotion, in the guise of a visitor about to conduct a sight-seeing tour. Yet the authority of the priest over K. is such that on first seeing him he crosses himself and bows, 'which he ought to have done before'. As K. attempts to leave, he is called back by the priest, and it is significant that the word 'mighty', so rarely used by Kafka, is used here to describe the voice which calls: 'A mighty, practised voice. How it penetrated through the cathedral, ready there to receive it.' After a moment's hesitation K. races back to the pulpit from which the priest has spoken—'with long, flying steps', as though in a dream. The completeness of his submission is shown by the violence with which he throws away his tourist's guide on being asked whether it is a prayer-book.

The gist of the sermon or parable which K. now hears is too complex to be paraphrased accurately, though clear enough when read in full. In the main it is concerned with the possibility of entering in at a gate, and with the question of necessity. All of it has obvious reference to K.'s case: it explains, in brief, why he has not himself entered the gate appointed for him. Perhaps the most striking thing about it, however, is K.'s reaction to it. After raising some objections, the last of which is never fully met, he becomes resigned to the necessity which the priest has outlined; he no longer feels himself in a position to confute, but accepts the element of mystery. 'He was too tired to survey all the consequences of the story, and the trains of thought into which it led him were unaccustomed; they were unreal things, better suited for discussion among the society of court officials than by him.' K. recognizes here the transcendence of the court as his namesake recognizes the transcendence of the castle. Perhaps he also recognizes that the question of guilt and innocence is, like the question of acceptance and refusal, not primary. The last words of the priest to him are, 'The court wants nothing of you. It takes you up when you come and releases you when you go.' K.'s belief in his own guilt or innocence is a matter of necessity: the court exists to reflect these beliefs, to give them a context. As he is told earlier, the court is 'attracted towards guilt'. But it never of itself accuses him. Thus, while K.'s guilt is real enough, it is not his business to justify or condemn it, but rather to accept it as inevitable. 'One doesn't need to take everything to be true,' says the priest, 'one must only take it to be necessary.'

It is the recognition of this necessity which surely gives K. his calm demeanour in the final chapter, where his death is narrated. Apparently sentence has been pronounced, and K. is condemned. Much depends on how this final act of the court is regarded. It may appear as a last display of senseless hostility towards K., a punishment meted out to him alone, whereas others are spared it. Or it may be seen as representing the sentence of death to which everyone is subject, and which the court in time pronounces equally on all. That does not make death any the more sensible, or reveal any truth about it. But the choice remains open: to regard it as retributive or as necessary. K., for his part, is clear in his attitude. Having seen Fräulein Bürstner for the last time he is aware of his guilt. At the same time he becomes resolved not to offer any further resistance to his captors, and this very act of consent brings him a measure of happiness. (This is perhaps the only time in the book that any such feeling is ascribed to him.) 'He started walking, and something of the happiness ['Freude'] which he thereby gave the gentlemen passed into himself.' I am reminded here of Kafka's phrase: 'There is no way. What we call a way is only a long hesitation.' K.'s hesitation has been replaced now by resolution; he has not progressed along any way but is suddenly at the end of it, and at the end there is even happiness. His continuing reflections show further signs of his changed attitude.

"The only thing I can do now," he said to himself, and the conformity of his steps with those of the two others confirmed his thoughts, "the only thing I can do now is to retain to the end my calmly dissecting reason. I always wanted to plunge into the world with twenty hands, and moreover for a purpose which cannot be approved. That was wrong. Shall I show now that even a trial a year long was not able to teach me? Shall I leave like a man who has been slow in the uptake? Shall I let them say of me that at the beginning of the trial I wanted to end it, and now, at its end, I want to begin it? I don't want people to say that. I am thankful that I have been given these half-dumb, un-reasoning gentlemen (his executioners) on my way, and that it has been left to me to tell myself all that is necessary."'

In this brief moment K. experiences regret, recog-nition of wrongdoing, submission to the court's au-thority, and even gratitude to it. To defend himself now would be, as he says, to begin the trial all over again, just as in *The Castle*, if K. were to insist at the end on knowing whether the documents in his case were really destroyed, he would place himself back in his earlier state of challenging scepticism and lose the happiness he now has. It is only because K. is in step with the court, or at least with the two officials it has sent to him, that he feels his present attitude to be confirmed.

It is a hard end, despite the comedy of the two executioners in their top-hats and their ridiculously considerate ceremoniousness. K.'s last words are even desperate. 'Like a dog', he said; it was as though the shame should outlive him.' Yet at least for a moment Josef K. has experienced something of the harmony felt by K. in the taproom at the Herrenhof. It lasts for a shorter time, and it does not translate itself into feelings of good will; it is a seed which has no chance to bear fruit. But the seed is present, and as somebody (I think it was Max Brod) has already said, *The Castle* could scarcely have been written without the experience of *The Trial* to precede it.

The nuances of both these novels cannot be fully expressed in the paraphrase which any commentary must be. One can only offer a line of approach, and leave it to the works themselves to express their own total meaning. Yet the least forceful nuances are sometimes the most powerfully suggestive. Thus even the desperation and shame of Josef K.'s last moment is modified, not only by the memory of the person who suddenly appeared with outstretched arms at a window, as K. lay waiting for the knife, but also by the possibility of resurrection. Does Josef K. believe in or hope for it? It has been seen how, in *The Castle*, when Pepi offers K. hospitality in her subterranean room, he is quick to take up her suggestion that he at least will not always be bound to it, and that spring returns at long intervals. In *The Trial* there is a remark perhaps related to this. As Josef K. is making arrangements to conduct a certain Italian gentleman on a sight-seeing tour of the cathedral, he is puzzled by one of the latter's remarks. The Italian is indeed somewhat mysterious: one suspects at times that he himself is an agent of the court, sent so that K. shall arrive in the cathedral to hear his appointed sermon—at all events, once the arrangement has been made the Italian never appears again. The remark I am referring to occurs at the first greeting between him and K. 'The

Italian shook K.'s hand vigorously and laughingly called somebody an early riser.' The narrator adds that K. did not understand whom he meant—though in fact K. has risen particularly early that morning. 'K. did not understand whom he meant, and it was in any case a strange word, whose meaning K. guessed only after a little while.' What is strange about the word, given the circumstances? Did it refer to K.? When did he in fact guess its meaning, since it is never referred to again? Did he guess before or after his early death? Did the Italian say the natural thing under the circumstances, or did he intentionally drop a hint? The doubts continue after the final sentence of *The Trial* has been read.